CUNT

versus

PUSSY

an incomplete
CONFESSION
in rough DRAFT

M. Jane Colette

This novel is entirely a work of fiction.
The names, characters and incidents portrayed in it
are the work of the author's imagination.
Any resemblance to actual persons, living or dead,
events or localities is entirely coincidental.
Oh, wait. Ooops. No. This is a work of non-fiction.
A *faux* memoir. Fuck. It's mostly true.
Except for the parts where I lie. But for the record,
I mostly lie accidentally. When I plan to deceive,
I tell you I'm engaging in an evasion or omission.
Which makes it ok, right?

A Rough Draft Edition, for Beta Readers Only
GENRES were made to be BROKEN

@mjanecolette
tellme@mjanecolette.com
facebook.com/mjanecolette2
goodreads.com/mjanecolette

Submitted to Library and Archives Canada
Cataloguing in Publication

ISBN: 978-0-9958102-0-4
e-book ISBN: 978-0-9958102-1-1
printed and bound in Canada

mjanecolette.com

For you. Of course. Who else?

For Debra

with sparkles
twinkling toes,
pistachio cream
desserts, and...
& so many other
sweet things!

marzena /
m jane colette

CONTENTS

Part 1: CUNT versus PUSSY...1

an interjection FOR AN INVITATION...207

Part 2: TEASERS...211

Part 3: A VERY USEFUL APPENDIX...229

EPILOGUE: Math sucks but it doesn't matter...258

ABOUT THE AUTHOR: evolution of a bio...259

PART 1

CUNT *versus* PUSSY

MANAGING EXPECTATIONS:
I'm writing for YOU but I'm a liar

CUNT VERSUS PUSSY began as a gift to my amazing beta readers—you—who wanted to know the story behind the story—and whether it was true that the most contentious negotiating point in my first publishing contract really centred on the word 'cunt.'

(It did. More anon. *Ad nauseam.*)

So. This story-behind-*that*-story is for you.

Because, when you asked, of course I had to tell you.

Because my work wouldn't exist without you.

In fact, I'm not sure *I'd* exist without you.

See, I have this theory that art isn't really art until it's shared. It's my version of that saying, "If a tree falls in a forest and there's nobody around to hear it, does it make a sound?"

I think it doesn't.

I think... it didn't even really fall.

Events need a witness; art needs an audience.

What do you think?

Tell me.

Somewhere along the way, what was supposed to be an honest-(mostly)-but-amusing story of how a (dirty) novel gets published and sold in this Brave New World morphed into a coming out story of sorts and then a personal-and-professional manifesto about why I want to write filthy,

dirty books, and, by extension, why you should read them…
or, better yet, write a few of your own.

You're welcome.

As you're reading, there's one thing you need to keep in
mind. Everything a writer gives you to read—even if she
claims it's non-fiction, memoir, and nothing-but-the-truth—
everything she gives you to read is a crafted narrative.

A performance.

(Never forget that.)

Still, this is as honest and truthful a performance as I can
manage right now. There might be a few white lies sprinkled
in, and some strategic omissions. I've tried to be honest
with you when I engage in them… and if you want to call
me on them, please do.

I want you to treat this story as a dialogue. I wrote it for
you, after all, and I'm telling it to you—*just to you*. If you
have a question—if you need a clarification—ask me, and
I'll do my best to answer.

And I promise to lie only when it's absolutely necessary.

Because I am trying to be truthful—you have no idea
how fucking hard that is for a fiction writer—most of the
chapters are structured as Confessions. But there are a lot of
interruptions. Questions. Interjections.

Every single one of them is your fault, by the way.

But we'll get to that.

Ready?

Let's manufacture a beginning to the story, shall we?

CONFESSION 1:
So I write this dirty, dirty book...

WHAT HAPPENS IS I'm pacing in my kitchen, laptop open, going mad. A client is about to make the biggest possible strategic fuck-up ever, it's going to ruin my career, my reputation, my life, and I can't stop it. I am pacing, swearing, going crazy, completely off-kilter, and I'm pretty sure the world is about to end.

Ping.

My phone. A forever friend. You know? Maybe you've made them in grade one. Maybe in high school? Mine are from university. Spread now across four continents. Still my most important loves. He's coming to town, first time in two years. Dinner? Yes!

In my Facebook feed—a story about the phenomenon of Facebook divorces.

I'm in my kitchen, laptop open, going mad... Facebook divorces... forever friend. I won't write back, not right away. I'll enjoy carrying him in my pocket.

Oh.

I like that.

I really like that line.

I stop pacing and I write it down.

(This is how poems happen. Apparently, novels, too. But I don't know that yet.)

Message from the client who's about to ruin my life and her business. Urgent.

What if…

I won't write back, not right away. I'll enjoy carrying him in my pocket.

Oh. That's a good line too. Suppose I…

Could I?

Maybe?

The phone rings. I let it. I'm too busy spinning a story…

Could I? Should I?

The. Phone. Will. Not. Stop. Ringing.

Fuck. I answer.

It's the client. I'm trying to save her, but she does not want to be saved…

As I talk to *her*, I'm carrying *him* in my pocket. But now he's in my head. What if… and how about? I can see him now—no longer *my* forever friend, but *her* forever friend. No. *Her* forever lover. Your forever lover. *First* lover? Old boyfriend? That archetype… And what if… and could I? I can see him so clearly, what I would want him to be like, and I wonder… could I show him just through *her* eyes? Your eyes? And then, I wonder… can I show him just through text?

Ping. He texts, again.

Will you have time for dinner while I'm in town?
—But of course.

He will ask… or she will ask—"With our significant others?" But she won't mean it. She definitely won't. And so… is that how it begins?

Maybe.

I start writing.

I manage to keep the client from committing the biggest strategic fuck-up ever. Save my career, my reputation, and my life. All the while, a little distracted, because…

I'm writing.

6

I see the rough story arc that first day—I see where it has to peak, and where it has to crash (twice, it has to crash twice).

I also see that I don't know how to do this. I don't know how to pace and to hold something that big in my head, so I must take a short-cut. And that short-cut—my scaffolding—will be the structure. Thirty days. Thirty chapters. A chapter, a day at a time.

How much easier can it get?

I know, also, that I can't sustain the tension I want to create over more than thirty days—it will only work if the timeline is compact—this is not a happily-forever-after fairy tale ending—this is an excerpt from life... I want it to feel real and it will only feel real if...

I write.

I write in fits and starts. In fifteen and twenty minute increments of time, snatched from the demands of daily life. An hour or two here. An hour or two there. I write between assignments-for-pay and children's speech therapy appointments. I write at parties.

Him: Who's that weirdo with the laptop in the corner?
Her: Never mind her. She's having a mid-life crisis and thinks she's writing a novel.

I start writing on December 3, 2012.

By January 1, 2013, I have skeletons of all the chapters. I know what's going to happen, and when. More or less, anyway. I continue to add, flesh out, throughout January.

Then I crash. Completely.

I write nothing in February. Not a word. I work. I do kids, life.

Also, I angst. I fire clients, take on new ones, and wonder what the fuck I'm doing with my life.

In March, I decide that while I don't know what the fuck I'm doing with my life, what I'm *going to* the fuck do with my life is finish this stupid book. I lock myself in a hotel room in the mountains for two days and one night. When I'm done, I have 75,000 words.

Half of them, I think, are sequential…

I write in April. May. It's easy now. I know where I'm going, what I'm closing, what I need to flesh out, what I need to add. I am so close to being done.

I 'finish' on May 6, 2013. I remember, precisely. May 6, 2013. The story has a beginning, middle, and end. It flows. It has purpose.

It is so fucking dirty, what the hell was going on in my head?

Her: It's the post-weaning hormonal rebalancing.

—What? I stop breastfeeding and I turn into a raging slut?

Her: Pretty much.

Ok. As good a theory as any…

Is it good? Is it bad? I don't know. It's done.

Or is it?

I give it to him, to her, *to you* to read.

I run to the mountains—the mountains and I, we have a thing—and I lock myself in a hotel room again, this time for three days and two nights, and I rip it to shreds.

Mostly, I take out words.

I rearrange a few scenes. I add nothing. I take out a lot.

You text me while I'm doing that, do you remember?

Holy fuck. I just finished. What did you do? How did you do that?

I preen.

I think… half of it is pretty good.

The other half… Christ. What demons was I channeling?

And how the fuck am I going to show this to my husband?

My parents?
OMFG... are my children going to read this one day?
Whatever.
None of that matters.
I have written.
It is done.
Six months.
About 100,000 words.
Ready to be read.
What next?

FIRST INTERRUPTION:
Whoa, whoa, whoa...

THAT'S IT? THAT'S the great reveal on how you wrote Tell Me*?*
  —Yes.

I was hoping for… I dunno. More?
  —Well, there is more. You've got dozens of confessions to go, beloved! But the writing really is the easy part. When you have to write… you just do it. You sit your ass in a chair—on a couch—on the floor—and you do it. There is no short cut.

Well, but there's got to be some coaching. Practicing. Advice?
  —Sure. We're gonna get to that. Sort of. Bear with me. Right now, we've got to find my dirty book a title.

CONFESSION 2:
You tell me the title really sucks

I'M TERRIBLE AT titles. Always have been. My working title for the novel is *30 days in the life of a cyber-adulteress.* Classy, right?

Then, I get really, really high class and snobby. *The New Colette.* Because, you know—Colette? Sidonie-Gabrielle Colette? Author of *Gigi? Cheri?*

I do apologize. I thought I was being so clever…

You said, do you remember, you said,

Sapiosexual is not a synonym for snobby. Jesus, woman. Who's going to want to read that?

I said,

—I HATE YOU.

And I cried.

The first batch of readers got *Tell Me* as *Perfect Trust.* There's a riff in the book, you know, where Marie demands of Jane whether she knows what perfect trust is? I thought it fitting…

But then… *You* read it. Finally. And I was so excited you had. I couldn't wait to hear.

—Tell me. Fuck, tell me! What do you think?

I texted. We never talk, do we, you and I? We text. Words on a screen. You said, do you remember?

Tell Me.
—What?
I think the title of the novel should be Tell Me.

Oh, fuck, yeah. Why didn't I see it?
Tell Me.
I typed it into the title page of the manuscript.
It was perfect.
And it was your idea—not mine.
Thank you.

CONFESSION 3:
And then, I get hit by a truck (it's a metaphor)

WHEN YOU READ writers writing about writing (and you really shouldn't, right? You should just sit your ass in a chair and write), you'll read about their *hindsight insight* into the process, into what they think makes them tick... unless, of course, you're violating their privacy and reading their journals and letters.

Which we really shouldn't do, should we? What do you think? Is not reading a letter not written for you, reading a journal entry that was a howl of pain and a personal conversation between a human being and her demons—is that not an act of ultimate personal violation?

Says the woman who has all of Anaïs Nin's diaries on her Kindle.
—But I feel really bad about it.

Maybe there, in those letters and diary pages never meant to be read by strangers, there is, occasionally, a sliver of truth about how writing really happens, really works.

But, generally? **Hindsight insight is worthless.**

With that caveat... this is what happens to me and to *Tell Me.* You know those dreams, when you're standing in the middle of a busy city intersection, naked?

Yes.

—Good. If you had said 'No,' there would have been this awkward silence, and I'd have to rewrite the whole next part...

So. It's June 2013. June 22, 2013, if you like precise dates. I'm standing, in the middle of a busy city intersection. Fully clothed. Cloaked, in fact, in medieval armour. Impenetrable. Ok, maybe a chink here and there, a bit of a structural weakness developing with age. But generally, oh-so-safe. Confident. Protected. Bold.

My armour is my past. My career. My professional successes to date. My marriage, thirteen years in the building. My community. My roles, my masks, my story of myself.

I like my armour.

It means I·can stand here, in the middle of this intersection... and feel sale.

Cars, trucks, cyclists, and the occasional pedestrian whizz by me. I watch. Not moving, because I'm not sure where to go. This way? That way? And how? I'm not paralyzed, mind you, I'm not frozen: I'm just in this space of utter anticipation. *Anything* can happen. Until I move, all is possible. And I'm enjoying the moment; it is intoxicating.

Terrifying... but intoxicating.

I did it: I wrote a book, *my book.*

I started. I finished. What am I going to do next?

Cars. Trucks. Cyclists.

And... then... holy-mother-of-god... what-the-fuck... instead of whizzing by me the way all the others have, this yellow Matrix (2002, I think, the rear windows tinted, why?) heads straight for me and I stare at it in shock and horror (time does slow down) and wonder if I should, you know, jump? But there are other cars everywhere too... no, I'll just stand still—as I stare at it in shock and horror, out of the corner of my eye, I see a Vespa (burgundy, gorgeous, its scratches artfully hidden), also on a collision course.

And then, none of it matters, because before either of them gets to me, I get completely and utterly flattened by a massive Optimus-Prime-type truck. Carrying nothing but water…

(Stupid metaphor. Forgive me. But it's my confession, so I can craft it anyway I like.)

The Matrix and Vespa ride over the wreckage. It's ugly. The Vespa, I think, tears my lungs, intestines to shreds, but at the time, I hardly notice—that pain will come later.

Right now, I'm mostly reeling from being hit by that truck.

Full of water.

What the fuck happened? Aren't you going to tell us what happened?
—No. Because it doesn't matter. Insert your own personal tragedy-train wreck here. I'm trying to show you the process: the details, in many ways, interfere. Let me sketch broadly. Sketching broadly versus drawing meticulously, specifically, forces you, the reader, to fill in the details, to complete the picture—to make the story your own. It's more powerful.

This is a gyp.
—It's a metaphor.

You are a coward.
—Well. I won't argue with that, yet.

The worst thing—that book, *my* book? That moment full of potential, anticipation, joy, pride, all those things? Gone, gone. I can't find it. I don't care about it. It can rot, wither, die for all I care—I care about nothing.

When I get up from that intersection, finally, I am broken. And naked. All my armour gone. Also, possibly, my skin.

So. I do nothing.

Nothing.

Here's my hindsight insight: so, granted, there was that unexpected Optimus Prime truck encounter. But even minus that... I bet you I would have done nothing for a while. Just without the excuse. Because fallowness inevitably follows output. You know? You create—and then you crash. You give birth—and then you're drained.

Also... that moment of anticipation, all-potential (pre-rejection): so nice.

Sometimes, I wish I could stand there again.

Anything could happen.

Nothing is risked.

CONFESSION 4:
Six days crafting a five sentence bio

WHEN NOTHING IS risked, nothing happens.

A year later, I'll realize I was reeling from severe PTSD. (That truck, never mind the Matrix and the Vespa, was really big.) At the time, I just feel stupid. Lazy. Hazy. Unmotivated.

I experience the world through a fog.

I force myself to do something about the book in September 2013. Here's the thing: maybe I should re-read, revise it. Right? That's what people do to drafts. They keep on reworking them.

I can't, I can't. I can't bear to look at it. Think about it.

I need to... Ok. I need to find an agent. Right. And then they'll do all the work for me. Yes. So. I need to put together packages, queries.

Fuck.

So much to do.

I feel overwhelmed.

I need... one task, a tiny task.

Something easy.

Got it.

I need to write a bio.

I can't.

I suck.

My entire life and career up to this point have been pointless, meaningless, and are completely unprintable, impossible to articulate, ridiculous to put into words.

Never mind, of course, that I have a CV, a professional online profile, a list of letters after my name, an assortment of awards and recognitions, an enviable list of publication credits. Even previously published poetry and fiction.

None of it matters. It's worthless.

I am worthless.

Fuck.

I weep.

I weep to him, and he gives me panaceas and I hate him. I weep to her, and she tries to fix me. She offers me solutions. She even writes drafts of the bio for me, and I resent her. I weep to you and you shrug, and say…

If you don't fucking believe in yourself, who will believe in you?

And I hate you (a lot).

And it doesn't help.

I weep some more. I drink too much.

She tells me, "Why is this so hard? Just be yourself."

She uses the word 'authentic' and I throw a clay pot at her.

I write two, three, six, *sixty* versions of the same, very bad, five-sentence bio.

I will never, ever get this together. I will never, ever write a good bio that sells me, captures me, vaults me into the hallowed halls of authorhood.

Fine. I won't. **I'll just write a crappy bad one that does the job.** Name. Credentials. Intention.

It's awful and pedestrian. Except when it's pretentious.

No matter.

It's done.

DIGRESSION: *Irving Layton on poetry, orgasms, and academics*

IF POETRY IS like an orgasm, an academic can be likened to someone who studies the passion stains on the bedsheets.

Irving Layton

ORDERS: Have a non-academic orgasm with a poet. A prose writer with stellar cadence is an acceptable substitute.

CONFESSION 5:
The first pitch

THE NEXT THING I need, apparently, is a synopsis. How fucking boring. And seriously, a synopsis? For this book? No.

(This, by the way, is an example of self-sabotage. If every goddamn literary agent's and publisher's submission guidelines ask for a synopsis: write a fucking synopsis. My hindsight insight: this is September 2013, and I am very, very broken, and it's not even that I can't do anything right—I don't want to do anything right. I just sort of fake-move through the process. With minimal effort.)

So, instead of writing a synopsis, I craft a pitch. I distil from the submission guidelines the commonalities... and I realize none of them really matters. The thing I need to do is grab attention. Aggressively. Quickly. Because otherwise no one is going to make it to the third paragraph, let alone the second page.

(I have some experience in this type of work. Most of my clients have Crackberry-induced ADD. They can't make it to the second line of an email, never mind the second paragraph...)

So. I pitch.

*

Dear Mr. X,

Re: *Tell Me* (103,000 words)
Genre: Up-market women's fiction/Raw erotica

I'm a veteran Canadian business/legal affairs writer looking to sell my first novel, and your agency was recommended as a potential good fit for me and my project by [one of my clients].

Pasted below my signature line is a synopsis of the novel and a brief biography. The manuscript is complete and ready for consideration if the synopsis piques your interest.

I thank you very much for your time and consideration, and look forward to hearing from you.

With pleasure,

M.

*

Confession-within-the-confession: the client's name I dropped? So here's the funny thing. You'd think after writing professionally for nearly twenty years, I'd have some connections in the publishing world, right? Nope. *He* is the only person I know who might possibly-maybe be recognized by an agent in the Canadian publishing world. Maybe. He wasn't too sure about it, and neither was I... What he actually said was:

You can use my name in vain all you want to. Not that I think it will help you any. I spent most of my career just pissing off people.

Still. I wanted someone to read past the first paragraph. All's fair, right?
Maybe.

Anyway, the name dropping? Didn't work. Didn't help. The story of selling *Tell Me* is most definitely *not* the story of 'It's who you know.'

FOR THE RECORD:
A bad synopsis can be a decent pitch

JUST TO BE absolutely clear here—this is not a synopsis. This is a pitch. But at this stage, I'm stubbornly refusing to write a synopsis.

*

Tell Me by [Me! Except I'm not M. Jane Colette yet]
(103,000 words)
Genre: Up-market women's fiction/Erotica

HIM: It's The Story of O *meets Jane Austen for the texting generation.*

ME: I'm not sure that's a compliment.

HIM: It is. Completely. Although you should have warned me what it was about. Flying coach with an erection is so declassé.

ME: I did tell you. I said it was one-third erotica, one-third chick lit, one-third existential angst.

HIM: Well. I didn't expect it to have quite this much of an impact. It's impressive. Tight. It flows. So very easy to read, and keep reading. The sex reads true. Don't call it chick lit. It's something different, new.

It's not a bad review, I think. Except... I didn't write it for him. He's not my target audience. I wrote it for—his wife. The woman who wants to be his mistress. The divorcing forty-year-old who reads pulp romances on the subway even

23

though the predictability of the plots bores her. The snobby sapiosexual who devoured *Fifty Shades of Grey* and still has it on her Kindle... but tells everyone how badly written it was. The Wall Street executive who wears French lingerie under her Armani suit and fantasizes about going down on that hot bike courier in the elevator. The faithful wife who wants, so very, very badly, to take a lover. But won't. Or will she?

I wrote it for them—that sprawling demographic of 35-50+year-old women who buy more books than anyone else, for whom new genres and never-ending series are created.

So, I give it to them to read, to test-drive:

So shocking! So awesome! Tell me—what does Matt look like? I need to know.

Your book. I can't stop reading. I was late for work today. Again.

God. I WANT HIM. How did you do this?

They're texting me as they read. I love it. But then I worry. Have I been able to sustain it? The storyline is compact: an intense love affair—although the lovers don't call it that, they call it a mindfuck—between the two central characters unfolds over thirty days, the tense and holiday-intense month of December. But that's thirty chapters, 100,000 words. Was I able to keep the pace, commingle the disparate plot lines, and keep the reader obsessed all the way through to the end?

Yes. Yes, I was.

Your book. I am having trouble working. I just want to take my phone into the bathroom and keep reading. I can't wait until lunch time so I can continue. Just finished chapter 24 on my way to work. Yes, I read at every red light!

It's 4:30 in the morning. I'm done. Holy fuck that's hot.

No! It's over and I don't want it to be! Tell me there's more!

Maybe. I have a second novel plotted out. But first I have to sell this one: *Tell Me.*

In short: Jane's a wife, mother, daughter, friend. Mostly content. Mildly bored. Suddenly, a text from an old lover pulls her into an online sexual vortex. As she 'mindfucks' her lover and attempts to figure out how this side of herself fits into her current life, other relationships around her fracture, implode. Her best friend is recklessly pursuing affairs of her own, while another friend is struggling with the fall-out of an ugly divorce. Her next door neighbour is planning a wedding with her forever on-again/off-again lover—but will it really happen? Her parents, on the eve of their forty-third wedding anniversary, announce they're getting a divorce. Her father-in-law leaves his third wife—no, wait—she left him... And her lawyer husband—is it just business texts he's exchanging with his associate? Does Jane care? Should she? Or is she too engulfed in her sanity-straining mindfuck to think?

Throughout the book, the relationships change—cross-over—strain, collapse.

Survive.

It's uber-sexy. Well-written. Highly consumable. The erotica is undiluted and un-euphemistic; the characters are engaging; and the life plot lines as real as if they were happening to you, your neighbours, your colleagues.

It's going to make someone a lot of money.

So.

Tell me.

Do you want to see the manuscript?

*

What do you think? Good? Bad?

Irrelevant.

Done.

I end, of course, by appending that terrible bio.

Her: I want to see the bio!

—It's really not worth seeing. I promise.

AN INSIGHT: J. Jack Halberstam on why it's important to write stories that don't end with the cum shot

FIRST, CONSIDER THIS:

The wedding is the 'cum shot' of romantic comedy.

and this:

...no one likes a sensitive man, mouthing some truism he overhead his wife say while sneaking off to watch Internet porn.

and this:

We may all know, see, and acknowledge the clichéd quality of the romance plot, but until we are raised with different understandings of love, desire, and intimacy, we must still cleave to it, still long for the happily ever after, and still find ourselves disappointed and devastated, stranded at the altar like a jilted bride who believed that marriage would make her happy but discovered that, like the wedding, marriage is overpriced, overvalued, overestimated, and maybe soon, simply over.

J. Jack Halberstam, *Gaga Feminism*

CONFESSION 6:
Mail it out, throw up—repeat

SO. THE FIRST pitch is done. Cover letter, the thing that I'm pretending is a synopsis. A bad bio.

And then? Yeah. I act. I send out a dozen, more email packages.

Then I vomit.

No, really. On hands and knees in the bathroom, puking.

So afraid. It's out there. I've done the thing. I await judgement.

I feel sick.

Two hindsight insight lessons from this confession.

First, in the words of Julia Cameron:

...students come to me hoping to lose their fear. They believe 'real artists' are fearless. ...I teach them to have their fears and create anyway. 'Real' artists are people who have learned to create despite their fears.

Yup. Nothing to add to that. Create despite the fear; move through the fear.

(This, by the way, is a lesson I intermittently forget, need to relearn.)

Second, you know the people who say,

I tried to find an agent...

I tried to get it published...

But it's just impossible...

Ask them how many queries they sent out. Always.
One? Not enough.
Four? Ha.
Fourteen? You're just getting started.
Forty? That's a girl. Keep on going.
I lose count at forty-seven.
I feel sick, and end up on my hands and knees puking in the bathroom, every single time I hit the send button on a new batch of queries.
It just doesn't get easier.
At all.

CONFESSION 7:
OMFG she knows a publisher?

WHILE I'M IN the middle of mailing out cold queries—
puking, and when I'm not, just wanting to, you know?—
she emails me, and says, "Are all your revisions done? Are
you done and ready to show it to other people? Do you
want me to send it to my friend the American publisher?"

Whaaat?

Squeeee!

Yes!

What? You need to interrupt me again? Go ahead...

*Janest? Loveliest? There are a lot of he, she, you in your stories.
D'you think you could give them all names?*

—No. Two reasons... First, reality is fucking messy.
Really. It has too many people. And the reader can't keep
track of them. Is she talking about Cheryl? Or Lisa? Janine?
Or Lara? Paola? Or Cathy? Jenn? Or Sabine? Nicole or...

—See? Her. She. It's better this way. Trust me.

—Second... names... names have power. Suppose, for
example, I told you her name was Cheryl. And Cheryl's the
name of the girl who broke your heart in grade five—your
nasty boss—the androgynous clerk at Safeway you have a
mind-affair with. You're no longer thinking of my Cheryl,
experiencing her as I need you to experience her. You're
mixing her up with yours. That's why, by the way, so many
of the names in romance and erotica are so ridiculous.

Writers strive to find names without any negative associations to them. My strategy—did you notice it when you read *Tell Me*?—is the opposite. Names as plain, as common, as unimaginative as possible... stark, minimalist, evoking as little as possible, until you get to know them...

—So... no names. She, he, you. Them. Ok?

Do I have a choice?

—No. I'm a control freak. And I'm controlling and scripting this narrative. But keep on asking questions—I don't mind being interrupted, most of the time. Now where was I?

Squee! She knows a publisher!

A few words about *her*: she is one of my life's beloveds, because she lives her life with courage, integrity, determination, and a passion and appetite for all things rainbow. We are so different, she and I, but in the core things, the same. Our first bond was motherhood: her child was born a few months after one of mine, and our relationship was formed in the forge of sleepless nights, bleeding nipples, and the most terrifying life change the human animal experiences.

She always thought I should write a book about motherhood and parenting.

So. It went like this.

—I did it! It's finished!

Her: What? What? Oh-my-fucking-god, you finally wrote a book!

—I finally wrote a book!

Her: I. Need. To. Read. It!

—You! Will!

And—because in her I have perfect trust, and no fear of harm or judgement or harsh criticism, I send it to her.

She's Beta Reader 1.

31

I neglect to explain… I forget to set up… I don't tell her what *Tell Me* is about.

She thinks she's getting a book about parenting.

Ooops.

She survives. Just barely.

And then…

Her: Do you want me to send it to my friend the publisher?

Yes, yes, a thousand times yes.

Wait, wait. Stop. You, over there. I see you. There you are, going,

Ha! I knew it! It's all about who you know!

It isn't. Let me save you the suspense: her friend the publisher never gets back to me. Never acknowledges the receipt of the manuscript, never even tells me "Not interested." Never tells me anything.

She's heartbroken, and feels she's let me down.

I'm ok. And of course she hasn't. It was a chance, it was a risk—it didn't play out.

Onward.

I do ask her,

—But, oh, beloved… did you tell the publisher what kind of book it was? Or were they thinking they were getting a book on parenting?

Her: It sort of is a book about parenting. Motherhood.

—And sex.

Her: Well. Sex is the first, essential step towards motherhood and parenting, right?

True. But in our Madonna-Whore culture, we manage to forget that, entirely.

CONFESSION 8:
Cock tease—or, I don't get an agent

ONWARD. MORE PITCH packages, more emails.

I'm targeting Canadian literary agents, because... patriotic? Something like that? Need to start somewhere? And I start with the handful in Montréal, because I love Montréal. It's the place I first pretended to be a writer. The place I took my first massive professional risk. The Canadian city that I think best understands me.

And... he bites!

Remember? That first pitch? It worked. He writes back in six hours!

Very good pitch.

Enough to make me want to read the first twenty pages if you grant me an exclusive for one month.

If that works, please email the material and in the subject line put MATERIAL REQUESTED.

Thanks...

I get the message on my phone while on a rocky beach with two of my loves and my children, and we are undignified and we scream and dance and we all think,

This. Is. So. Easy!

And they say,

You. Are. So. Talented!

And I think,

Nyah-nyah-nyah, all you 'it takes six to eight months to get a response from an agent or publisher' people, my book is going to be in print by Christmas because I. Am. Awesome!

(Don't mock me for my delusions of grandeur. They are so fucking brief. And the crashes afterwards, so bad.)

I go home. Email him the first thirty pages (I know he asked for twenty; I'm not that good at following instructions, have you noticed? The first thirty pages take him to the end of Chapter 1/Day 1... and *I* don't want to be a cock tease. I think that's just wrong). Put the children to bed. Celebra-fuck. Drink wine. Forward his message to everyone who's read *Tell Me*. We all have a "Woo-hoo!" cyber-party.

I'm excited for three days.

And then, he tells me he hates.

He hates me.

Well, he hates the book.

Ok, maybe hate is too strong a word.

He writes:

Thanks for sending this material. I'm afraid I'm going to pass. I found the writing to have lots of energy, but right now, for me at least, it is a bit too scattered to come together. I wish you all the best with this, and thank you for allowing me to see it.

Best wishes...

No, he hates me.

Did you see that?

He just said I won't amount to anything.

I want to die.

34

Ok, I don't. But I want to drink, to excess, and it's 10:30 in the morning and I'm a mother.

I cry to you.

You just need one yes. This is just the first no.

Right. One yes. First no. Onward.

Onward.

Do you want to hear how many 'No's' I get? Can you take it?

(Can I?)

CONFESSION 9:
Rejection blows goats

THE FIRST NO. The second no. I lose count at forty-seven. The way I tell the story, now, is I say I was rejected by every literary agent in Canada, and half the American ones, but I suppose I exaggerate, just a bit.

I can't quite decide which are worse. The form "We didn't really bother to read past the first paragraph despite demanding that you spend two hours tailoring your query to our specific demands" letters? The personalized "Interesting project, but not a right fit for me, but best of luck, I'm trying really hard to be kind to you, do you notice?" rejections?

Actually, it's this one:

Great pitch. Really interesting project. We'd encourage you to pursue self-publishing and see if you can hit a few thousand in sales and then come back to us.

Because: really? If I can do that without you... what the hell would I need you for?

I utterly run out of steam and desire to do anything on the book by March 2014. I. Am. Done.

Confession-within-confession: I am also crazy. No, really. I am still reeling. I'm not thinking clearly. I'm not capable of strategizing. Of evaluating. Of planning. I'm treading water, doing things: sending out submissions randomly, not learning much from the experience. Not putting in the five hours of research that would save me five months of rejection and pain. I am engaging in subtle sabotage. It *looks* like I'm doing things... but I'm not.

I'm treading water. I'm wallowing in existential angst.

To get release... I fire clients who annoy me. I am incredibly, brutally selfish with lovers.

I drink too much, lie to my therapist, and when I want to cause myself a little more pain and angst—I send out yet another query to an agent who's clearly the wrong fit for my work.

Occasionally, though, I come alive for a few minutes and engage in acts of reckless brilliance...

THIS EXPLAINS A LOT:
Erica Jong on the writer's 'fuck you' impulse

THERE IS IN *writing—or any creative work—a kind of fuck-you impulse. Part of the energy comes from sheer rebelliousness. I'll show you! a writer says. I am not who you think I am.*

Erica Jong, *Seducing the Demon*

CONFESSION 10:
'If at first you don't succeed, maybe you shouldn't try sky diving'

RECKLESS BRILLIANCE. OR desperation.

I'm done with agents. So done with agents.

I should... I should start reaching out directly to publishers.

Like, look, this one. Open to submissions again. Vancouver press. Small but kinda' daring.

Not too literary.

Should I?

The internal dialogue goes like this:

—They wouldn't touch my work with a ten-foot pole. Let's face it, I didn't write a book. I wrote porn with a plot.

The Me Pretending To Be You: Just fucking try.

—I'm so tired.

The Me Pretending To Be You: Of what? Achieving nothing? Do it. What have you got to lose?

—I'm so tired...

But I also have this really great idea for a new pitch—it comes to me in a flash—it's offensive, and it's untrue, and it's absolutely brilliant.

Ready?

*

HIM: Hey, I was on the [Publisher] website the other day, and they're accepting book submissions again—you should send them Tell Me.

ME: I saw that too. They also say they take forever, their office is tiny, messy, and poorly managed. And there's some crack about them being not too bright. I'm unenthused.

HIM: I met [Editor's Name] at a party once. I think. The night's a bit blurry... But. He's actually quite clever. Even by your sapiosexual standards. And he'd be totally into your book.

ME: Mmmm, I looked at their book list in some detail. I like what they've published, and I've read a bunch of it—although, I read everything, so that's not much of a yardstick—but I'm not sure I really fit.

HIM: You wrote a dirty book that's mostly about existential angst. What is it that you're calling it now?

ME: You're calling it *The Story of O* meets Jane Austen for the sexting generation.

HIM: Exactly. Smart, sexy, and consumable. They'll jump at it. Or at least masturbate a bit while reading it.

ME: Jesus. Nice pitch.

HIM: What have you got to lose?

ME: Ok, fine. I'll send it. Of course I'll send it. But I'm totally blaming you if they don't read it.

HIM: They'll read it. And... um... actually, don't use my name. If that was [Name] at that party I'm thinking of, I think I puked on his shoes.

Hi. Are you still reading? A PDF of the full manuscript is attached, but to save you the exertion of downloading the file if you're thoroughly uninterested, I'm pasting the pitch/synopsis and my bio below my sig line. (I have a password-protected online version of the manuscript available if you'd rather stroll through it like that. Let me know).

I look forward to hearing from you. Actually, to be perfectly honest, I dread the inevitable six weeks to six months of silence. Jee-zus. Don't take longer than that. No wonder writers drink. But I do sincerely appreciate your time.

Thank you,

M.

*

What do you think?

I dare use it twice. The publisher I craft it for never acknowledges receiving it. Silence. Yuck.

I recycle it for another. He gives me the courtesy of a response:

Thanks for sending on your energetic pitch letter and manuscript sample. I'm afraid we're going to take a pass.
Good luck in finding a suitable publisher.

The moral of this story is... I haven't a clue. Is there a moral? I think maybe it's this: doing something is better than doing nothing. Do I mean that? I don't know. In many ways, I think if I had just done nothing between June 2013 and June 2014... I'd still end up in the same place. What do you think?

I have good news, by the way. We're finally getting to the part of the story where I stop being crazy and SELL the goddamn book.

Thank god.
—You're feeling grateful? Imagine how I feel?

PS This Confession's title is taken from a quote in Susan Harrow's *Sell Yourself Without Selling Your Soul: a woman's guide to promoting herself, her business, her product, or her cause with integrity and spirit.* It's a nice book. It still requires you-the-woman-with-integrity to, you know, DO the work of selling herself... and ugh. Hard. I read it while I'm trying to develop the marketing plan for *Tell Me...* don't implement any of her suggestions.

My Left Brain: You are so lazy.
My Right Brain: You are so whiny.
—Some Other Part Of Me: You know what? I'm trying to figure out how to do something totally unnatural here. Some help and support would be appreciated...

Her: Are you talking to yourself?
—Sort of. It's a right brain, left brain, Gemini thing.

You: And the whining about selling and marketing? Is that an artsy-fartsy artist thing?

Um... Well... I don't know. I'm not sure. At this point in the story, I am not thinking of myself as an artist. But yeah—I find the process of selling myself, framing myself, pitching myself—packaging myself and my work as a product—extremely distasteful.

And that is... a problem. And a limitation.

Plus, I'm still crazy.

But, not for much longer.

CONFESSION 11:
I fall in love by the river and stop being crazy

IT'S RAINING, AGAIN, and he's breaking my heart—maybe I'm breaking my own heart, yeah, that's probably a more accurate description of what's happening—and I'm very, very tired of treading water. Of being crazy. Of being—listen, listen, I love this phrase—an architect of my own suffering.

Jane 'thinks' this phrase in *Tell Me*, but she stole it from me; this phrase first came in a text, do you remember? I wrote it to you when we were existential-angsting one day, and I said,

—I've come to realize I'm pretty much the sole architect of my own suffering.

and you said,

Isn't everyone?

and we got all Buddhist and insufferable, and I was a little cheered up, for a while. But I didn't stop. Because there was pleasure, pay-off in continuing the suffering.

One day in June 2014—the anniversary of that 'I get hit by a truck' incident—**I decide to stop being the architect of my own suffering.**

Yeah, it's that easy.

Not.

I decide to give myself a deadline. One more month of treading water, of being broken. And then: for fuck's sake, woman. Move. Think. Plan.

Right.

Watch me go...

No, actually, really, watch me go... except, what happens, is this.

Three things.

First, I fall in love by the river. I'm sitting in the middle of an unflooded river bed with another broken writer, and I describe to her the book I'm *not* working on right now (but dreaming about… and I really only put it into words for her because I want to impress her), and I tell her about the book that's finished that I'm doing fuck-all to sell, because it's terrible-no-good-and-who-would-want-to-read-crap-like-that-anyway, over-saturated market, and she says,

Osprey!

...and I have this moment of river-sky-bird-freedom-words.

And she says,

You HAVE the chops to do it.

And she's talking about the book I'm not writing, but I start to think about the book I've written, and I lean in and kiss her and I fucking soar, I think I'm going to be an osprey, I'm going to hunt again...

("Artists need other artists," Julia Cameron counsels in *The Artist's Way*. I'm no artist, I dare not think of myself as one. But in that moment, in that moment: I need… you. You know? **I need you to read me**. If you don't do that, if you don't complement me, complete me, then I don't exist.

44

Does that make sense? In the middle of that riverbed, it does.)

I am primed to act. Almost ready to do the work, I feel it, but, what? Am I scared? Maybe scared. Because, fuck, rejection. Rejection is hard. And I am exhausted. Spent. Not really healed from June 2013 and all of its fall-out, sorry-for-myself, drinking too much.

So... Second: I stop drinking wine. Really over-do it on the caffeine... Stop sleeping... I am a bundle of nervous, un-channelled energy that has to go somewhere.

Her: Have you read Julia Cameron's The Artist's Way?
—Sounds fucking pretentious. Anyway, I'm no artist.

Her: You might find it helpful. Right now. Or, you know. You can just stay bat-shit crazy and unproductive forever.
—Fuck you. I'm working. I'm doing all the things I have to do.

Her: Well. But you're not writing. Anyway. Just a suggestion.

Third, I meet *her* **on a loading dock between two garbage cans,** and she takes me up to her studio. And she is an artist, and she lives and breathes her art and I don't know what it is she does in the process of showing me her canvasses and telling me about her clients, but I fucking fly out of her studio, I cannot wait to get home, I shed hat-scarf-shoes as I run through the hallway, I fly to my desk, and I write.

Mostly, about the truck. A little about him. You. Her. Life. It's chaotic. It's life. It has potential. Doesn't it?

I feel... alive. I feel... courage. I feel...

I. FEEL.

(Here's the thing about getting hit by a truck: it leaves you so numb you don't realize you're numb. Until you're not.)

I open *Tell Me*. I read it.

45

To be perfectly frank, I come a couple of times at my desk, with no additional stimulation.

Fuck.

I did this. I dreamt this. I wrote this. I made it real.

I am going to sell it.

IMAGINE THIS:
Susan Sontag and Ernest Hemingway
in a conversation about sex (and writing)

EASED OFF ON the book...in May because Dr. said I worked
too hard in April, and May fine month to fish and make love to Miss
Mary.
   I have to ease off on makeing love when writing hard as the two
things are run by the same motor.

Ernest Hemingway, *Letters*

Hmmm. And what do you say, Susan?

If only I could feel about sex as I do about writing! That I'm the
vehicle, the medium, the instrument of some force beyond myself.

Susan Sontag, *As Consciousness Is Harnessed to Flesh:*
Journals and Notebooks, 1964-1980

Writers in the audience: what is your mind-body
relationship when it comes to creativity and sex? Can you
fuck and write at the same time? (You know what I mean.)
Do you need to alternate? Does one use up energy for the
other?
My feelings about sex and writing are all mixed up. Or
maybe that's the wrong word. Intertwined, inter-connected.
Feeding off each other. Hemingway said writing and
'makeing love' (that's how he always spelled making, by the

way, isn't that awesome?) were powered by the same engine and if he wanted to do one, he had to ease off the other. I find fucking makes me want to write, and writing makes me want to fuck.

...and if I were writing this for a creative writing class, the homework I would give in this moment would be:

—Writers, this weekend, go fuck the way you write.

Oooh, you should totally do that. And, lovers of writers, demand that performance.

CONFESSION 12:
The results of five
(actually, two) hours of research

I HAVE A plan.

The plan: Find a publisher for *Tell Me*.

It is July 8, 2014. Almost six months left in the year. So, if I do not have publisher by the end of December, I will research self-publishing.

(Your take-away: **Deadlines.** It's the only way anything gets done, ever.)

Step one: Buy *The Canadian Writer's Market, The Novel and Short Story Writer's Market*, and, oh... what's that? On the shelf right next to it? *Writing and Selling Erotic Fiction?* Awesome. After all, what I wrote is really more porn than literature. And I'm ok with that. Because, lover, have I told you? **It's fucking amazing, and there's no other book like it in the world and it's MINE.**

Step two: Identify publishers from *Canadian Writer's Market* and *The Novel And Short Story Writer's Market* that will accept unsolicited manuscripts. Oh, fuck. Of course. High brow literary presses one and all. They will not touch me with a ten-foot pole, oh-wait-what-about-this one? And this one? Ok. Let's try these two. What do I have to lose?

(I'm still thinking local. I think it's because I was born before the Internet.)

Step three: Have a minor meltdown.

Id: Do Canadian publishers just not want to make money? Do they only accept boring high brow stuff no one will read? Where the hell do I fit in these stupid categories?

Super-Ego: For fuck's sake woman, you wrote a dirty book. Target the erotica publishers and stop pretending...

Id: I have not been pretending!

Super-Ego: You so have!

—Ego: Ok, maybe a little. But see, I didn't set out to write a skanky book.

Super-Ego: I know. But you did. So. Who published Fifty Shades of Grey? *Who is Sylvia Day's publisher?*

—Ego: I don't want to be in that company.

Super-Ego: Suck it up, princess.

Id: Why are you so mean to me?

(Yes, I fight with myself in my head ALL THE TIME. Sometimes, on paper. Occasionally, I'll do it out loud while walking. It's why my children refuse to go for walks with me now that they're sentient. Also, I think Sigmund Freud might have been a Gemini.)

Step four: A list of eight publishers, only one of them Canadian, to target. And, a new pitch. Wanna hear it?

Awesome.

Actually, it's not that different from the old pitch. It's just way shorter.

*

Dear [Publisher's Name] Editors,

I'm pleased to submit for your consideration my erotic novel, *Tell Me* (100,000 words). The attached two documents contain a detailed synopsis of the novel and a three-chapter sample of the manuscript (the first, the sixth, and the epilogue chapters). The synopsis includes a summary of the novel (also pasted below), as well as its cast of characters, an outline of the key relationships and plot lines, a table of contents and some teasers of the sex scenes and prose, a formal 'pitch,' and my biography—in which you will find out I'm a seasoned Canadian business writer looking to place my first work of fiction.

But indulge me, for a moment, and let me introduce *Tell Me* this way:

HIM: It's The Story of O *meets Jane Austen for the sexting and blogging generation.*

ME: I'm not sure that's a compliment.

HIM: It is. Completely. Although you should have warned me what it was about. Flying coach with an erection is so declassé.

ME: I did tell you. I said it was one-third erotica, one-third chick lit, one-third existential angst.

HIM: Well. I didn't expect it to have quite this much of an impact. It's impressive. Tight. It flows. So very easy to read, and keep reading. The sex reads true. Don't call it chick lit. It's something different, new.

I hope you agree.

A more conventional summary: Jane's a wife, mother, daughter, friend. A couple years shy of forty but not stressing about it... yet. Mostly content. Mildly bored. Suddenly, a text from an old lover pulls her into an online sexual vortex. As she 'mindfucks' her lover and attempts to figure out how this aspect of herself fits into the obligations of marriage and motherhood, other relationships around her strain, fracture, collapse. Her best friend is recklessly pursuing a series of cyber-affairs, while another friend's attempt at an open, polyamorous marriage leads to an ugly divorce. Her next-door neighbour is planning a wedding with her forever on-again/off-again lover—but will it really happen? Her parents, on the eve of their forty-third

51

wedding anniversary, announce they're getting a divorce, while her father-in-law's third marriage ends. Meanwhile her lawyer-husband is exchanging a lot of texts with an adoring young associate. Does Jane care? Or is she too engulfed in her own sanity-straining mindfuck to really notice?

Thank you very much for your time and consideration.

Jane Colette

*

Hit the send button.
Vomit.
Repeat.

QUESTION:
Was Sigmund Freud a Gemini?

ANSWER: NO, SIGMUND Freud was not a Gemini. He was born on May 6, 1856. So, Taurus.

He must have had some Geminis in his life though. That whole Id-Ego-Super Ego theory? So Gemini.

Oooh. Speaking of Geminis, check out these two books:

Erotic Astrology: The Sex Secrets of Your Horoscope Revealed by Phyllis Vega

and

Sextrology: The Astrology of Sex and the Sexes by Stella Starsky and Quinn Cox

So. Jane. Astrology. Whazzup with that?
—Nothing. Totally not my thing. Thought you'd find it interesting. That's all. Um... so... what's your sign, anyway?

CONFESSION 13:
How NOT to write a synopsis

I SPENT A year not providing agents with the synopsis they asked for, because it didn't make any sense to me. That is, giving them the type of synopsis they wanted was not going to give them a sense of the book. Of me. Of what we could be.

(Hindsight insight: maybe the lack of synopsis was part of the reason for the initial swack of rejections? Maybe? Just maybe? I plead: insanity. PTSD. A year of living in fog and *sans* critical thought.)

But this time, I was doing things *right*. Determined. They want a synopsis? I'll give them a fucking synopsis.

I need to find out what a synopsis is.

Research.

Fuck.

Seriously? This is what they want? This is *not* how they are going to taste *Tell Me*.

Ok. Let me think. How can I give them what they think they want while actually delivering what I need them to see...

Aha.

Like this:

First, a Summary. Easy. That's basically the 'in short' blurb from my first pitch.

Next, a Cast of Characters. Names. Ages. One sentence descriptions.

Ok, now... Key Relationships and Plot Lines. That one takes a while. Wow, I packed a shitload of stuff into this book.

And then? The publishers want spoilers. So. How It All Ends. Everyone's 'happily ever after' ... ok, so there's not a single such thing in the book. But the romance genre has a word for what I did. 'Happily for now.' Which is all we can ever hope for, no?

Next... A Handful of Reviews. Quotes from you. And her. And him.

Thank you, by the way. I don't know if I can say it often, loud enough.

THANK YOU.

Now what? A Sampling of the Sex Scenes. Grrrr.

I go down between your thighs. Licking. Biting. Tongue thrusting. It's been a long time since I've done this—these days, I prefer to watch you while you play with yourself. Or to fuck you so hard you scream. But, mmmmm, this is nice. You're delicious. The smell of you is intoxicating.

And... A Taste of the Prose. A fairly sex-free part. (Yes, there are some).

Next—About the Author. The bio. Still lame. But I don't care.

And... Contact Information.

There.

Done.

The beast hits twelve pages and 3400 words. It breaks ALL the rules.

FUCK, YEAH:
Breaking rules works

BREAKS ALL THE rules, yes.

But guess what?

It works.

Three of the eight pitches elicit a response...

But, I don't know that yet.

Right now, I've just pushed 'send' on the new batch of pitches and am, again, vomiting.

You'd think it would get easier.

It really doesn't.

CONFESSION 14:
'So... may I see some more?'

I BRACE MYSELF for rejection, and it comes. Although, man, it's the loveliest rejection letter I've received to date:

> *Jane—we had a chance to look at* Tell Me, *and while your writing is compelling and the story great, it's not a good fit for our core of romance-centric readers, because of the infidelity angle.*
>
> *Just because we aren't interested in acquiring this manuscript doesn't mean we aren't interested in seeing further romance works from you. We wish you much luck in finding a home for your manuscript and hope you'll consider [Romance-Focused American Publisher Who Wants to Offer Readers Only Sin-Free Fantasy] for future romance projects.*
> *T.*

And maybe I'm sturdier now, too? Because it doesn't really hurt. And I think, I can endure more. I send T. a happy thank you for the lovely rejection. She writes back:

> *I think that's the best thank you for an 'r' I've ever received. And I was serious, if you write something that hits more of the traditional romantic tropes, I'd love to look at it!*

It's almost like a thumbs up, right? I can endure seven more of this (I've sent out, you may recall, eight pitches).

But oh-holy-mother-of-god, I don't have to.

On July 22, 2014 I had pitched *him*.
And, on July 29, 2014 I get this:

Thanks very much for your proposal, which I look forward to reading. Will do my best to read your work soon.
Kind regards and thank you for thinking of Mischief.
A.

Form letter made to look like a mildly personal letter, right? Whatever. I file it mentally under "I'll never hear from them again." I don't care.
(Liar, liar, of course I do.)
Except... HE WRITES BACK TWO DAYS LATER!
He says...

Dear Jane,
I hope you are well. I've really enjoyed your sample chapters and the unusual outline—never encountered one like that before, but it certainly presents the ideas in a more interesting way.
What I like most about this proposal are the circumstances and situations: married people, with children and jobs, behaving like twenty-somethings in social media, which they do/must do. It's very unusual for ER/romance, or at least what I see as there are so many trends and sub-genres. The weight of what Jane and married characters have to lose, and have in their home lives/professional lives creates a tension you don't get with singleton characters chasing billionaires (99% of what I am sent these days). The fears for secrecy and discovery just work for a storyteller. The rule of thumb in erotica, from way back, was not to include domesticity because it was a passion kill switch, but you've the ability and ideas to bypass that prejudice with this story and these characters. So I applaud the freshness and novel approach.
I have a bias against text message/email affairs, because they are usually poorly executed and dull, but the one between Jane and Matt is very edgy and sexy. I read the proposal first, because I didn't want to know how this flirtation is resolved—she and Matt make a go of it,

but how would that affect the children?, she and husband revive their relationship through an affair (has happened), Matt turns out to be an immature disappointment ... lots of possibilities, but actually none of the above really, so it's good to create curiosity but confound expectations too.

So, can I see some more?

Best,

A.

Cue hyperventilation. I forward the message to you, him, her, them.

You write back:

Harper-fucking-Collins?

At which point I go, what? Because... Mischief. Didn't he say Mischief?

And you say...

Do you not see the goddamn email address?

Right. Mischief is an imprint of Harper-fucking-Collins. And I pass out.

...

My sane, Super-Ego self reminds me of the Cock Tease Agent Incident, and says, "He just wants more, he hasn't read the whole thing yet, this isn't your YES."

My Id is fucking screaming for joy. She is high, elated, drunk with glee, and, in this moment, she whispers, seductively, into my ear: "No one who matters has read the whole manuscript yet. He will be the first, and he will devour it—you know you just had to get someone to read it, you just had to get past the gatekeepers! This is it, this is your win, your first real reader..."

Him: Hey! What do you mean no one who matters? What about me? And him, and her?

—But all of you love me. Unconditionally. And some of you are sleeping with me. And others want to. So, seriously. Would you tell me it sucked?

Him: Yes.
—Liar.

And I send off the whole manuscript and I stop breathing.

True fact: you can live for two whole weeks without breathing.

Janest? I have a question.
—Yes, my beloved?

He's going to be the first one who matters to read the whole thing… so… wherefrom all those other tales of woe and rejection?

—Those were all rejected pitches, prepared for, mostly literary agents. And the rejections, most often, were based on just one page. That's all they demanded: one page. In some cases—"one paragraph, if that spikes our interest, we will ask for more." Sometimes: first ten pages, first thirty pages, first chapter, first three chapters, three random chapters. Often: a torturous, structured submission package that required creating new materials—that synopsis, of course. Bio. And, that all important pitch.

So. He's going to be the first.
—He's going to be the first.

Is he going to love it?

Wait. Wait.

CONFESSION 15:
I come on a mountain, literally

DO YOU REMEMBER? I said—it is possible not to breathe for two weeks. Finally... August 13, 2014.

A message. From HIM.

Oh-my-god, is there anything better? Worse? Anticipation. Potential. Hope. Until you click on the link...

I don't want to click, I'm afraid to click.

In a former-former less-solvent life of mine, I had learned to hate the look of my own handwriting. Before email and the Internet, rejection letters all came in self-addressed, stamped envelopes—you had to provide the means by which editors and publishers could reject you.

This is just a message.

An email message.

Nothing more.

Except... in this moment?

NOTHING ELSE MATTERS.

Ok.

I can do this.

Click.

Hello, Jane.

GASP. Well. If it's rejection... at least it's going to be personal, right?

Super-Ego tells me to be reasonable and calm. And she says: "Even if it's a 'No, thanks'—the pitch fucking works, you got a door open, you can use his first response as leverage to get other doors pried open, ok?"

Id: READ. THE. FUCKING. MESSAGE!

I read the fucking message.

Um. I don't get it. It's very long. I don't see any of the words. Maybe, I faint. I try again. Ok, it starts like this:

I've finished reading Tell Me *now, and I think this is a very inspired book and approach to the genre. So I really enjoyed the novel—it's frenetic and complex and often funny and very well observed. I came away thinking it's a* Desperate Housewives/ Sex and the City *but without the Cinderella glamour and make-believe. It's like social realist erotica and there isn't much of that around. Romance and erotica is usually really down on downbeat stories and characters, but this never felt downbeat or pessimistic, it felt vivid and uncomfortably well observed. No one really comes out of it well—they're all so flawed.*

If this is a 'not for us' kind of message, he's put a lot of effort into it...

Fuck, there's paragraphs, pages more. **But. What. Does. He. Mean. What. Does. He. Want. Does. He. Want. The. Book?**

I found Jane and her friends' secret lives and Jane's inner life slightly terrifying (and her duplicity), so good to get a bit of male panic going! It maybe uncomfortable reading for some, but that's a risk I always like in generic genres that just endlessly reinforce trad' aspirations.

It's a risk you like, but... is this leading to a but?

It's odd to me how few writers try and reflect on the recent social media and online dating/affair trends that have almost been a revolution and have often made middle-aged people behave like teenagers.

But. Are. You. Going. To. Fucking. Ask. To. Acquire. The Book????

My only constructive criticism…

Are. You. Trying. To Kill. Me?
Deep breath. I skim. Race word after word after word looking for… THIS:

Anyway, what are your thoughts? I am waiting around this time of year to talk to Avon about the new schedule for 2015, but I'd be very keen to have your book at Mischief.

And then… well, what would you do? Obviously. I grab you and we go and climb a mountain. And fuck on its summit. Because. Yes.
One. Yes.
I just need one yes.
And I think… did I just? I did. I just got it.
Yes.

INDULGE ME:
I really want you to read his entire 'I Want You' email, ok?

SO, THE ENTIRE message goes like this:

I've finished reading Tell Me *now, and I think this is a very inspired book and approach to the genre. So I really enjoyed the novel—it's frenetic and complex and often funny and very well observed. I came away thinking it's a* Desperate Housewives/ Sex and the City *but without the Cinderella glamour and make-believe.*

It's like social realist erotica and there isn't much of that around. Romance and erotica is usually really down on downbeat stories and characters, but this never felt downbeat or pessimistic, it felt vivid and uncomfortably well observed. No one really comes out of it well— they're all so flawed.

I found Jane and her friends' secret lives and Jane's inner life slightly terrifying (and her duplicity), so good to get a bit of male panic going! It maybe uncomfortable reading for some, but that's a risk I always like in generic genres that just endlessly reinforce trad' aspirations.

It's odd to me how few writers try and reflect on the recent social media and online dating/affair trends that have almost been a revolution and have often made middle-aged people behave like teenagers.

What's clever is how her sex life with Alex is re-energised through a fantasy affair that is always in danger of becoming real, and then does become real. You do realise you run the risk of readers hating Jane too? Again, it's a riskiness I like personally. I think the characterisation is post-modern rather than traditional genre, which is addicted to heroism and happy ever afters.

My only constructive criticism is how many characters and how much ground the story covers in their respective stories. The energy really makes the story forceful, but can be slightly exhausting once you're about half way through. Around page 170—the section with Alex's parents—made me begin to wonder if there was too much digression from Jane. Though all insightful and funny at times, I did wonder if the cast is too broad?

I also had to repeatedly check the dramatic personae you sent through so I knew exactly who was having an affair with who and which mum was which (I think a cast list of sorts would have to be included as this is a wide reaching suburban saga).

You have a trilogy's worth of material in one book, but the colloquial style and short sentences enables you to cover that much material in 100K words. Marie or Nicola or secondary characters being extracted might give the reader more time to breathe (increasingly, readers are becoming an impatient bunch), and characters coming in and out may not be so easy to distinguish.

That's not essential, just a suggestion. It's also tempting to test readers' reactions with the unabridged, full-length version.

The ending also kind of drifts to a close—there is no real resolution or HEA [happily ever after], or cliff hanger, but I wonder if that could be more dramatic or tense and possibly suggest a continuation of the maelstrom? Or a greater suggestion of the consequences that come with risk included earlier. I liked the bits when Alex seemed to have rumbled Jane, and as her judgement is impaired at times, it is possible that he would suspect more, or even know. So creating more enigma over that might work.

Only technical problem I foresee is that Avon are not keen at all on the word 'cunt'—has abusive connotations in UK. Would you be open to an alternative, like 'pussy,' particularly outside of the sextings?

Anyway, what are your thoughts? I am waiting around this time of year to talk to Avon about the new schedule for 2015, but I'd be very keen to have your book at Mischief.

Best, and thanks again for your patience.

A.

SOCIAL REALIST EROTICA:
a collaborative definition from Julia Cameron and me

PEOPLE FREQUENTLY BELIEVE the creative life is grounded in fantasy. The more difficult truth is that creativity is grounded in reality, in the particular, the focused, the well-observed or specifically imagined.

Julia Cameron, *The Artist's Way*, Week Four

Want some more homework? Today, observe your reality. Stare at it. From this angle, that. Now, choose a relationship—a dyad, two people, neither of them you—at the edge of your reality. So, not your parents, not you and your partner. How about—your neighbour and her lover? The two barristas, both tattooed, one pierced, the other not, at your favourite café? Your boss and her boss?

Now. Start crafting a fantasy. Write it down, or keep it in your head. The point: create a story (unreal) that could be real.

Effective fantasy MUST feel like it COULD happen. That's what defines good fantasy, good erotica, good sci-fi. It might be outrageous—there might be unicorns, aliens... but on some level, it's real.

It feels real.

CONFESSION 16:
My excessive attachment to the word 'cunt'

CUNT.

C-U-N-T.

C- - - .

When I say it, hear it, 'see' it written in my head, the 'c' is a very hard 'k,' and if I were designing the English language, I'd spell it kunt. The K-word, not the C-word.

I like the word. Like *bitch, whore, slut*—it's a powerful word, and because it's a powerful word, it's been co-opted to denigrate women.

I claim it, reclaim it, rub it all over myself, my work.

This memory, from when I was twenty-five, in an office in downtown Calgary:

Get that cunt out of my board room.

I didn't mind—I mean, I didn't mind being called a cunt. (I minded being told to leave the board room; and, no, of course I didn't leave.) I knew, even back then, that calling me a cunt was a recognition of my power as much as it was an attempt to take it away.

What I minded was when they called me... 'little girl.'

My new publisher (I have a publisher!) minds the word 'cunt.'

68

Only technical problem I foresee is that Avon are not keen at all on the word 'cunt'—has abusive connotations in UK. Would you be open to an alternative, like 'pussy,' particularly outside of the sextings?

So, here's the thing.

No.

If I was thinking pussy, I'd write pussy. There's a reason I chose cunt, why Matt says cunt, why Jane...

Her: It's not a deal breaker. Don't be a stubborn idiot. Change it to nail the contract. Then when you sell an obscene number of copies, you can use it in the second book.

Confession-within-confession: the working title of the book I'm writing while negotiating to sell *Tell Me* alternates between *Methadone* and *Love, Lust, and the 'C' Word*. (Right now it's *Consequences*. Or... *Defensive Adultery*. More anon...)

C for cunt.

And there's a total cunt motif in the book. Because...

...well, because cunt-slut-whore are powerful, powerful words. And I want to use them.

...and, ok, I realize I'm a little whacked that this is such a big deal to me, but it is.

You sigh, exasperated.

You should listen to the publisher and follow all his suggestions. They know what they're doing. Except on cunt. Don't budge on cunt.

I know you're being facetious. But I also know that you agree with me on why it was the 'c' word and not the 'p' word.

Other potentially offensive words that occur, *ad nauseam*, in *Tell Me*: cock, fuckslave, mindfuck, whore, slut. Those are all ok.

But the c-word for women's genitalia...

—No issue with clit?
A: Clit's fine.

Books have been written about this. (E.g. Naomi Wolf's *Vagina;* Inga Muscio's *Cunt: A Declaration of Independence.*)
Confession-within-confession: I'm massively amused that this is one of the key points in our negotiation.

—Cause that's the kind of high-class book I wrote.
Him: I expected no less of you.
—Pussy sounds so fucking infantile.

You get tired of hearing me whine about this ("I don't know what other word to use!"). On the plus side, so does my publisher. I think I push A. over the edge with the suggestion that I use c---.
(In the original manuscript of *Tell Me*, cunt appears 176 times. Imagine the effect of 176 c---.)
(Wait. That number seems excessive. Let me check it. Ha. So—sixty-seven times.)
(Cock, on the other hand, 126 times. Interesting.)
(I'm a little disappointed in myself, actually. I thought there'd be more cunts. No. Only sixty-seven.)
(Still too much for HarperCollins-Avon-Mischief.)
In the end, we effect this compromise:

A: Use 'c' word sparingly. Avon have outlawed it, but one or two tactical placements can work.

When I deliver my 'final' manuscript, it has seven cunts in it.
They let me keep four.
Small victories.
So. When you read *Tell Me?*
Pretty much every time you see 'pussy'—think 'cunt.'

CONFESSION 17:
A really bad contract

AFTER WE CLARIFY the cunt situation, I wait to get the contract.

And wait.

And wait.

You'd think, really, I'd be used to it by now—the waiting. I'm not. It's awful and frustrating. And December is a-coming—it is only four months away, and I think *Tell Me* is a Christmas book, really, and so...

I wait.

I prod.

Response:

I am at the mercy of an overworked contracts dept. I sent in the deal memo two weeks back so am waiting on a draft contract. Have just tried to hurry them up. But I'm still as keen as mustard about Tell Me.

(He really wrote 'keen as mustard.' It's because he's British. Apparently, they do say that.)

I wait some more...

Finally, on October 21...

I'm delighted to finally attach a contract.

I'm delighted to receive it. Thrilled beyond anything. It's a standard contract, my editor tells me. "All of the text is standard to Avon and Mischief authors."

It's kind of incomprehensible to me.

Except. Well, this is clear: They get:

- *all the rights to everything for all time*

while I get

- *no advance, and*
- *royalties of 7.5% of net receipts on physical format editions, 25% on digital editions to 10,000 copies sold, rising to 50% thereafter, 10% on physical audio format, and 15% on digital audio format.*

Beyond that, it's incomprehensible—and I don't even know if the royalty rates are good, bad, or standard.

Help.

Him: Lawyer, lawyer, lawyer. You. Need. To. Get. A. Lawyer.

Lawyer. Right.

I know a lot of lawyers. But much as I don't like to write for free—or ask a dentist friend for a freebie cleaning or check-up—I don't want to ask for this kind of work as a favour. So, I go to a non-friend expert, who, being a decent human, bends over backwards to make the process efficient for me, but it still costs a fortune—so much that I'll need to sell 1000 e-books before I recoup the cost.

She identifies for me all the problematic clauses in the contract.

There are many.

She tells me which ones, no matter how much I dislike them, are not worth fighting over, because it is unlikely the

publisher will budge on them. They're unfair to authors...
but they're standard, across the industry.

She tells me what handful to focus on.

I send A. an email entitled 'her outrageous list of demands.'

He 'manages my expectations.'

I cry.

In the end:

Lawyer: Well, you have to consider... are you going to fight them on the details or are you going to trust that they're going to be good people?

Right?

Also.

It's Harper-fucking-Collins. My first novel, however filthy, is going to be published by Harper-fucking-Collins.

I mean, surely that means something, is worth something?

In the end, I mostly give on everything. But I get to keep my film rights.

Note from future self to past self: should have asked for the audio book rights too. What were you thinking, woman?

Past Self: I was thinking big.

—Future Self: And you thought you'd have better odds of selling screen rights to this thing than having an audio book made of it?

Past Self: I was just so happy to have a contract. A publisher. I mean—Harper-fucking-Collins. Nothing else really mattered, you know?

(There's a moral in there, but I won't beat you over the head with it.)

Point: Contract. Executed on November 26, 2014.

I. Am. An. Author.

I should throw a party.
Instead...
I proof.

CONFESSION 18:
I can't find any typos

THIS IS ANOTHER boring part.

Confession-within-confession: I love writing and I have been a writer all my life, and professionally, for money, since I've been seventeen. I can't imagine doing anything else—I don't think I'm capable of doing anything else, actually.

But writing-as-a-career has a lot of really hard parts... and a lot of really boring parts.

Proofing is one of them.

I'm supposed to deliver a 'clean' (*i.e.* cunt-lite) manuscript to HarperCollins on December 2, 2014.

My much-adored A. doesn't ask for any substantial edits beyond suggesting I ramp up the tension between Jane and her husband towards the end of the book.

I fiddle with that a bit.

But mostly, I proof.

Truth: I fucking hate proofing.

I am not a line editor or copy editor. Going through *Tell Me* word-by-word with a fine tooth comb looking for lice— I mean, typos—is the most boring thing I have ever done, and I have written on some excruciatingly boring topics for my business and corporate clients.

By the time I get to the last page, I don't see any words. And I also hate the book.

I send it to her, one of my most enthusiastic beta readers.

—Can you read through this one more time, looking for typos?

Her: Of course!

A few days later:

Her: I can't do it. I keep on getting wrapped up in the story. And then masturbating.

—Seriously?

Her: Don't worry. No one will notice any typos if you missed any.

—Seriously?

Her: They'll be too busy masturbating.

I decide I should ask A. to provide me with a male, preferably gay, copy editor.

Grit my teeth, and read *Tell Me* one more time. Backwards.

Hate it. Horrible sucky book.

But—and this is what matters:

I deliver the manuscript on time.

It goes to A. With the message subject: 'proofed, edited and mostly cunt-less.'

INDULGE ME AGAIN:
He likes it, he still really, really likes ME!

YES! HE STILL likes it. Ha.

I've just finished my second reading of Tell Me, *and my thoughts haven't changed much, and neither has my enthusiasm for a book that is so different and engaging. I was more wary of the ferocity of the women the second time around. I'm ten years older than my wife, so you may have inserted a ripple of anxiety about the future. Overall, I think we are ready for copy edit.*

On balance, after reading the whole book twice, the only risk we run with the current version, and it's not a criticism, is that there is so much going on amongst so many characters, relentlessly. It is very rich and very intense emotionally and sexually—I like intense fiction—but the latter stages may lose some power as the same complex emotional ground is covered amongst such a big cast on 100K words.

Only place I could see to trim, I think I mentioned before, were the gym session on page 101–103, and maybe that and the way it entwines with the Colleen and Nicola material. Though this all does add to the world, the characters, and the story in smaller ways, but Marie and Lacey more than cover that range of feelings, as do Jane's insights. But, I know you're happy with this version, and I am not unhappy with it at all, so I think we can risk too many strawberries, and will go out with the whole vanity fair intact. I have also read it in two sittings—I think this is a book that should be read episodically, as in its narrative structure.

...I'm really excited to be publishing this, and will get the cover briefing and metadata up and dancing again. ...

Whoo hoo.
Whoop.
Squee.

CONFESSION 19:
I almost forgot to tell you about her (my) name...

SO. M. JANE Colette.

Just like the title was your idea, not mine, M. Jane Colette was the lawyer's idea. Well, sort of.

I had arrived at 'Jane Colette' as a pseudonym by the time I started shopping *Tell Me* around in the summer of 2014. 'Jane' for Jane Austen—in my opinion, the inventor of the modern novel and chick lit—if you haven't read Jane, pick up *Pride and Prejudice* or *Emma* today, and see how Jane's plot / pacing / conflict / climax / characters / conventions / tropes are mirrored in virtually every 'boy meets girl, boy loses girl, girl finds herself, boy realizes he was an ass, girl realizes maybe she was wrong too, ooh, happily ever after' book you pick up today, 200 years after Jane.

And 'Colette,' of course, for Colette, who took readers into the bedroom and boudoir in the most delicious French way...

Anyway.

Jane Colette. Isn't that a great name?

Sounds like a high class hooker.

—Go away. Well, ok. Maybe a little. High class hookers have the best names. So—a great name.

The lawyer provides these instructions: "Do a search to make sure there are no other authors with that name. And even if that comes up clean: add an initial. To make it more unique."

—What? Why?

Lawyer: It's possible there is a real Jane Colette out there. But the odds of there being an A. Jane Colette, or Jane L. Colette, for example, are much slimmer.

A. Jane Colette.
Jane L. Colette.
Well. There's only one initial that makes sense.
M. Jane Colette.
Done.
And that's how she—I?—came to be.

CONFESSION 20:
I'm not real

… AND THEN, AGAIN, nothing happens for a really long time.

Well, not true.

Life, of course, goes on.

HarperCollins acquires Harlequin, which causes a great deal of confusion at all of its divisions and pushes back *Tell Me*'s publication timeline.

Which is fine.

I need a little more time, anyway. Because sometime between the signing of the contract and Christmas 2014, I realize I've got a small problem.

Like… I don't exist.

I mean… **M. Jane Colette doesn't really exist.**

She is, at this moment, a name on a manuscript, nothing more.

I have to start creating her.

A few things are easy. I buy her (me?) a domain name, get her a gmail address, and a Twitter handle. A Tumblr placeholder. Wattpad? Maybe?

I have no idea what to do with any of these things, really.

Ok, not true. I don't want to make myself sound like a lame-ass luddite. My real self is a careerist and opportunist business writer, with a kick-ass LinkedIn network. She's been blogging for years, and she has a solid following and social presence. She knows how to create content and connect with people.

But see... she's real.

M. Jane Colette isn't.

She's a name on a manuscript.

She's a figment of my imagination.

She's giving me a nervous break down.

Him: D'you need to go see your therapist again?
—Shut. Up.

All the writers in the room: what do you do when you're paralyzed, confused, and have no idea what to do next?

That's right.

Research.

Ugh.

I don't wanna.

I really, really don't want to. I can't think of how to formulate the Google query, and how would I even judge the worth of the resources Google pukes up?

Research.

Or...

Ha.

Easier than research: whining to friends...

I whine about my angst, in a vague-and-disguised sort of way on Facebook (in a vague-and-disguised sort of way because M. Jane Colette is not only NOT real, she's a secret—this is a huge mistake, by the way—how the fuck do you promote a book, tell me, if you can't tell anyone you wrote it?), and the woman I fell in love with by the river and whom I still love, rescues me once again.

Her: The Right-Brain Business Plan*, by Jennifer Lee.*
—What?
Her: The Right-Brain Business Plan*, by Jennifer Lee. Try it.*

I try it.

Does it solve all my problems?

No.

But it gets me moving. And that is the most important thing of all, isn't it?

Momentum.

Moving.

The opposite of doing nothing; the only antidote to whining.

CONFESSION 21:
I'm not real... but I can create myself —and also, let me fucking whine, Dad!

MY DAD BOUGHT me my first typewriter when I was ten. He is so ridiculously proud of everything I do and write, it's almost embarrassing.

Anyway. As I'm struggling to figure out who the fuck M. Jane Colette is—and, really, in the process, who I am—he sends me this:

> *Here is my rant on your dilemma!*
> *There is this person, M.J.C, whom you've created.*
> *And now you do not know how to be her or how to animate her and she is dying.*
> *You do not want this to happen!*
> *People who were created by others have smarts, endurance, and live forever (think Sherlock) or much, much longer than their creators. And they become real. Look at Jessica Fletcher!!!*
> *What you need is a simple, multiple personality disorder injection or just admitting that you already were gifted with one or two personalities!*
> *So—here are the elements of your MJ makeover...*

Ok, I don't want to lie, but I need to paraphrase this next part to make it a little less embarrassing. My dad references the first novel I wrote when I was thirteen—a horrible pastiche about ethnic and drug gangs (cause I knew so much about that life, don't you know) after a three-week visit to New York. My three-continent childhood and what I turned it into. Academic trophies—I fucking kid you not—from junior high school. My first editorships and publications, and my long-forgotten martial arts career. Other professional achievements, and, most importantly, he says "your ability to focus, to be single-minded, and to get what you want."

Oh, Dad. I love you too. But, see…

Ok, you can read this part:

There is more to Jane than YYC! You have enough of your own material to make her exciting, bubbling, alive, and world-worthy. Plus you can throw in whatever you want! Fake it till you make it! Fake it real! No more doubts! No more public cries!

And the last word of my advice—you just need to fall in love and start loving all the people who live in you, yourself included!!!

Love You Always!

Your not so secret admirer!

PS Reply not expected.

Oh, Dad.

So much love, hey? I want you to know this, before you read the next part—so much love. I see it.

But here's the thing. This is my heritage, nature and nurture combined—the greatest thing my parents have done for me… and the worst thing they have done for me. Do you see it?

Message one: You are strong. You are talented. You are amazing! You can do anything you want!

Message two: Don't fucking whine.

You know what?

I want to whine.

85

I need to whine.
Whining is part of the process.
So thank you, Dad/fuck you, Dad.
And…
Actually…
There, he has a point.
I probably need to fall in love again.
M. Jane Colette needs to fall in love.
I'll add that to the to-do list.

QUESTION:
Wait. What happened to that woman...

...YOU FELL IN love with by the river?

Answer: It's complicated. Or not. She's not there, now—she hasn't been for a while. I am so grateful she came into my life when she did, though. I needed her desperately at that moment. (Just like you came into my life just when I needed you—thank you. And thank you, even more, for still being here.)

I am regretful she is no longer in it to celebrate the release of *Tell Me*, other things.

But. Mostly grateful.

CONFESSION 22:
Rantings of a Mad Girl
turned into a business plan (sort of)

THIS IS SYLVIA Plath. *That* poem:

> *I shut my eyes and all the world drops dead;*
> *I lift my lids and all is born again.*
> *(I think I made you up inside my head.)*

It cuts way too close to the bone these days.

I open up Jennifer Lee's *The Right-Brain Business Plan* and I start to do the work, unwillingly, resentfully.
It looks pretty. Nice design. Very girl.
Ok, princess. Suck it up. Do the fucking exercises.

Right-Brain Reflections
What will your plan focus on?
Primary: Promoting and selling *Tell Me*.
Secondary: Establishing M. Jane Colette as a brand.

Do you intend to ask for money?
Not asking for an investment from anyone—but yes, I want people to pay for the 'product'—the book.

Have you created a business plan before?

No. And I'm not... I'm having a lot of resistance to the process.

What intimidates you about doing a business plan?

It seems mildly distasteful. I'm a writer. I wrote the book. Someone else should sell it. Yes, I have clear issues about that here...

What excites you about doing a business plan?

Nothing.

Ok. Sorry. Bad attitude. I'll try.

I like the idea of building and having a road map. The creation of a new social identity. Having a sexy, skanky blog... the 'creative' things excite me.

What is you biggest challenge as an entrepreneur?

I don't like to sell.

I have a dysfunctional relationship with money.

What is your biggest strength as an entrepreneur?

I will jump off cliffs and out of airplanes. Without a safety net or parachute.

What's the most important thing you want to take away from this process?

I want to give *Tell Me* the best possible shot to be found, read, and enjoyed. I don't want to be passive about its success—I don't want to rely on the publisher deciding to put effort into it. I want to do everything I can to make it fly.

I don't know how.

CONFESSION 23:
I have no vision

JENNIFER LEE WANTS me to make a vision collage.

Sorry, Jenny.

Won't. WILL. NOT. And the guided visualization meditation makes me want to drown in the bath in which I decide to do it.

(I don't. Drown, I mean.)

Vision. Big Idea. That seems like an important thing to have, right? Let's think on that. Fuck the collage. But I'll write about it.

Writing, I can do.

Vision. What is my vision?

Big Vision, Right-Brain Business Plan

It's pretty simple:

> *SOLID sales for* Tell Me
> *leading to SUFFICIENT income*
> *that I can finish* Methadone, *write* Cassandra,
> *perhaps play with* Distraction Lover
> *and* Love Letters from the Flood Plain
> *TIME TO WRITE*

That's it. That's my vision: *Tell Me* is selling, and I am writing more. I am earning a living writing BOOKS, these new 'social realist erotica' books that change what people think about when they say chick lit or erotica.

EROTICA FOR THE DEMANDING MIND
EXISTENTIAL ANGST ON THE SIDE
ROOTED IN LIFE

Ok, that wasn't so bad. Kind of useful, actually. I now have a tag line for my author website, too. Erotica for the demanding mind, existential angst on the side. I like it.

What's next?

Fuck, Jennifer, another visualization? Really?

Bring your future vision to the present by using the present tense. Here are some prompts to help you:
I am proud of ...
It feels ... to have accomplished ...
I am honouring my values, which are ....
I set myself apart by ...

Ugh.

Her: Just do it.
—Fine.

Actually, these words come easily:

I am proud of my novels, and of the creative ways I've found to promote them.

It feels good to have written a book that speaks to real women's sexuality and eroticism and life reality.

I am honouring my values, which are motherhood-passion-action-courage-risk-'daring to look at the dark.'

I set myself apart by not flinching. By documenting, not fantasizing. By telling what is, not what could be if we had no responsibilities and if there were no consequences.

(Oh. *Consequences.* Could that work as a title for *Methadone?*)

My books will sell because no one has placed sex and erotica in this context before and
WOMEN ARE HUNGRY FOR IT.

Ok, that wasn't so bad.
It actually felt kind of good.

Jane? Clarification?
—Yes, beloved?
Methadone, Cassandra, Distraction Lover, *and* Love Letters from the Flood Plain?
—Later, later, later.

ON SECOND THOUGHT:
Maybe Sylvia Plath shouldn't be my role model

WRITING IS THE first love of my life. I have to live well and rich and far to write... I could never be a narrow introvert writer, the way many are, for my writing depends so much on my life.

Sylvia Plath, *Letters Home*

So true.
Except that she's so dead.
And I need to be so alive.

A COMPLAINT:
'Whoa, whoa, whoa!'

—WHAT, WHAT, WHAT?

If you don't tell me now, you'll forget! Methadone, Cassandra, Distraction Lover, *and* Love Letters from the Flood Plain. *Explain.*

—Right. Ok. It's really not important. *Methadone* is the second novel… Which I retitle *Defensive Adultery*… and then *Consequences*… and now… well, I don't know, which title do you like better?

—*Cassandra* was this idea I had while writing-not-writing *Methadone*: a woman inherits her 'psychic' mother's New Age store and falls in love with one of her clients, of course— right now, it's called *It's All In The Cards*, and I'd forgotten about it for a while, but I'm really excited about it again.

—*Distraction Lover* I junked. Bad idea.

—*Love Letters from the Flood Plain* became *Catalyst*, which I killed twice, but used a piece of it to seed what would become my third novel. I'll tell you a little more about some of them later, ok? But for now, you're getting ahead of everything and messing up my chronology.

Your chronology is fucked. And artificial.

—Well. Yes. But you're not supposed to notice, except for the moments when I tell you. Maybe… I think the important thing about those titles is—at the point at which

94

I'm trying to sell, launch *Tell Me*, I'm carrying in me the seeds of four more novels already. Isn't that awesome?

I don't need you to tell me. It is. I feel them inside me—and when I feel them inside me, I feel incredible.
Alive.

CONFESSION 24:
OMFG *not another creative visualization*

JENNIFER LEE IS determined to make me get my vision out of my head and out *there*. Somehow:

> *If guided visualizations aren't your cup of tea, here's an alternative exercise. Get a pen and paper and set a timer for ten minutes. Allow yourself to write freestyle about where you see your business and life in the future. Keep your pen constantly moving. Don't pause to think about what's next or stop to edit.*

Oh. This, I can do.
Timer set.
And… go:

*

In one year, I feel well on my way to having this second-third career as a writer-novelist. I don't think of my work as chick lit or erotica—it's just my work. People may still argue about it, aren't sure where to place it, but it doesn't matter. HarperCollins and Avon are fighting over who gets to be its imprint. Because *Tell Me* has sold 100,000s of copies, and *Methadone*—I'll probably call it *Love, Lust, and the C-Word*—is even better.

I get to use 'cunt' as often as I like in that book.

I have developed a marketing plan that works and that's creative and enjoyable. I love executing it. I also do it in the ebb-and-flow of what's really important to me—and that's writing the new books, and living a full, focused life, in which I am a present mother, a supported and supportive wife, a playful, rewarding lover, a fascinating, fun, and reliable friend.

I have a rhythm that works, that recognizes my creative cycle and its ebb and flow, that honours my periods of fallowness and turns them into something positive.

I have a creative support team to do those parts of the marketing I don't like to do. (Also, a housekeeper. Because, fuck housework.)

And, I am writing. I am outputting, revising, creating, dreaming. I see my projects through to completion. I find ways to distribute them and promote them that work—but what really sells them is that they are unique. No one else writes like this, talks like this, dares like this.

I write. I finish. I sell.

I am read.

I do all this against the backdrop of a real, full life.

I am fulfilled. Always, chasing, striving, changing. But fulfilled.

And, fulfilling.

*

My pen stops moving just as the timer goes off.

INTERJECTION:
Art, sex, imagination

ART IS THE sex of the imagination.

George Jean Nathan

. This, lover, *is* an order: This weekend, go hunting for sex of the imagination: for art—music, pictures, photographs (not that kind—porn's easy, go deeper), words.

This is a suggestion: If you're an entrepreneur—or a writer—flailing around for a vision, spend some time with Jennifer Lee on RightBrainBusinessPlan.com. Lee has two books out now—*The Right-Brain Business Plan* (2011) and *Building Your Business The Right-Brain Way* (2014).

They're very pretty, and easy to read.

A year from my first encounter with them—almost two—I will admit that they are also useful. If you do the fucking work they tell you to do instead of just reading them and doodling in their margins.

CONFESSION 25:
'Do you wanna shoot some porn for me?'

AMONG THE THINGS *The Right-Brain Business Plan* tells me to do is to identify my support network and my creative cohort, and to be aware of all the things in my tool kit. And, to use them.

Tool kit. Creative cohort. Support network.

Oh. In my tool kit, this:

I know some of the country's best photographers. And one of them is rolling into town in December to shoot some Very Important People.

I ask him if he wants to shoot some classy porn in-between as a favour to me.

Him: Oooh. Totally on my bucket list. How classy does it have to be?

—Well, I don't really want porn. But I want really, really sexy, evocative images. I want to create—I want this whole suite of images that captures M. Jane Colette. And a headshot. And some ideas I'll be able to send to the publishers for the cover.

Him: Who's M. Jane Colette?

—The writer. My pen name.

Him: So I'm shooting you?
—No. You're shooting M. Jane Colette.

Him: Who is not you?
—Well… ok, it's complicated, right? She's me-but-not-me. Look, just take the fucking photos, and don't make her look like me.

Him: Get a wig. Preferably red. I see MJ as a redhead.

Hmmm. Ok. Cool. Redhead. It's a long time since I've been a redhead…

The photographer and I decide that we should do the photo shoot in a hotel room in Calgary's Hotel Le Gervais, because it's one of the places mentioned in *Tell Me*.

Just because.

I buy wigs. A red one and a black one. And I get a little excited. Among the tools in my tool kit—I've worked as an artist's model on and off since my teens. I can hold the most ridiculous pose for the most ridiculous amount of time. And this, finally, is FUN. Playing and creating ART, and creating M. Jane Colette, and it doesn't feel like selling out at all.

You come with me to Le Gervais to give me whorish make-up, do you remember?

—Ugh, this is what I look like with red lipstick?
You look beautiful!
—I look like a caricature of Jennifer Coolidge!
She was never a redhead. Trust me.

I look like a cheap hooker in a cheap wig.

But I photograph well. And I don't look very much like myself. Which is the intent. I'm not, after all, real.

Not real.

But having fun.

And thinking... creating content for mjanecolette.com will be a lot of fun.

This offers me some relief.

Also... M. Jane Colette now has a headshot.

That makes her almost real, you know?

AN UNREMARKABLE MILESTONE:
M. Jane Colette's first blog post

THIS IS M. Jane Colette's first blog post. There's a moral embedded within. Don't look for it too hard—it kinda whacks you between the eyes like a psycho killer's sledge hammer.

*

January 1, 2015

Are you ready?
—Not even a little bit. I'm terrified, frozen, paralyzed, afraid to begin.
What are you going to do?
—Jump. Press publish, send, go. What else can one do?

And so, we begin. With... just, I think, this:

"Hi. I'm M. Jane Colette, and this is my author blog."

Her: But I think your first post should be really kick-ass. Powerful. You know? Stop the world in its axis and make it really pay attention.

—But if I do that, I will never do anything... my first post just has to BE. An outtake. Words on the floor. A promise of something to come. That's all.

Him: There are no readers for the first post anyway. It doesn't matter. It's a throw-away.

—Words on the floor.

Him: Precisely.

—And tomorrow?

Him: Tease again. And again. But be ready to deliver.

—I will.

*

Magazine and newspaper writing did not teach me how to write, publish, or market a book.

But you know what it taught me?

This:

An amateur thinks it has to be perfect. A professional knows it has to be done.

You're welcome.

No, seriously—if you're hoping to 'learn' anything from sharing this conversation with me... that, really, is the only thing I can teach you.

Finish shit.

Press send.

Publish.

Chasing perfection is the road to unhappiness; also insanity.

Done.

TORMENTING THE EDITOR:
Periods are over-rated; also, most people sext with one hand, not two

THE PROBLEM IS that A. likes periods:

> *...during the sexting, some messages end with periods, others are left unpunctuated. Though this probably captures the true nature of texts, we'll have to plump for periods, I think.*

I am a punctuation iconoclast:

—Periods: C'mon. Be cutting edge with me. Sometimes we text with full sentences and periods and sometimes we text with one hand all lower case breathless barely coherent because... it works better that way

—But if you're attached to periods, I'm not as attached to their lack as I was to the right use of the word cunt

(note absence of periods in this formal email to publisher)

(for the record, that email was written with both hands OUT of my pants)

(my fact-based argument for the omission of periods in most of the Matt-Jane text exchanges was that most of the sexting was one-handed if you know what I mean)

(I mean that he or she or both were masturbating)

(I just wanted to make that clear)

I make it clear—explicit—to the publisher:

—Having re-read chunks of the dialogue for the blurbs... I really think we should leave the texting punctuation as is. Because sometimes they're texting on phones and then it's sloppy, and sometimes they're typing to each other on laptops, and then, it's full sentences. And sometimes only one hand is involved...
—This will be how dialogue is written in the future, as we lose our ability to actually speak to each other.

A.'s note to copy editor:

Allow author to depart from house style in matters of punctuation.

Take that, periods.
Thank you, A.

TORMENTING THE COPY EDITOR:
Hyphenating 'g-spot' and other ways to make a grown man cry

FROM A:

> *Copy edit attached—it has light changes, though I have reversed the 'come' to 'cum' and am waving the house rules on that spelling to preserve the voice and intent as much as possible.*

Woo-hoo, woot-woot, squee.

I love that he's breaking all these rules for me.

Something to ponder: why is 'cum' so much dirtier sounding than 'come'?

'Make me come!' versus 'Now cum for me.' Totally different, right?

Now, unless you're a total word nerd, the following part will bore you to tears. Skim down to where I tell you to **START READING AGAIN.**

HELLO, FELLOW WORD NERD!

The HarperCollins/Mischief copy editor has nineteen queries. They are as follows:

1. Pg 2: Summary: Error! Bookmark not defined to be resolved. (Me: I'm pretty sure this is not my fault.)

2. Pg 8: First use of airport code YYC is in italic. Rest of texting line is not in italic. Take YYC out of italic? Not in italic in main text. (Me: I don't give a crap either way. Is this important?)

3. Pg 23: There are several references to 'thought crime.' Could use Orwellian *1984* 'thoughtcrime' instead. Is consistent though. (Me: My thought crime is definitely not Orwellian.)

4. Pg 25: Uses term 'thunk' as a sound. Suggest place in italic to emphasise this. (Me: Ok.)

5. Pg 14 onwards: Term 'Ping.' as a sound for Facebook alert appears several times. Suggest place in italic to emphasise this. (Me: Ok.)

6. Pg 59: Uses term 'whirr' as a sound. Suggest place in italic to emphasise this. Note that whirr can also describe the mechanical action as in 'The coffee grinder whirrs.' (p. 352) (Me: Ok, although this is getting tiresome.)

7. Pg 98: Text message from Jane: refers to four days ago, but events started five days previous. Amend? (Me: Wow, way to stay on top of things.)

8. Pg 99: Is 'Christmastifying' acceptable as a word? Would 'Christmasifying' be better? Hyphenated? (Me: I love creating new words.) (Obviously, I think Christmastifying acceptable as a word.) (But if you like Christmasifying better, I don't really care.) (Although that '-tify-' bit in the middle of the word seems very appealing.) (You know what, I don't give a fuck. Do what you will.) (Actually, use Christmastifying.) (PS I have no idea what ended up going into the book. If you read it and notice, tell me…)

9. Pg 128: Second line of texting (this is remembered texting, not real-time) only appears this one time and as such does not match up with other remembered text sequences which have been straight copies of text snippets. Is this ok? Line is certainly relevant to situation, but should perhaps be taken out of 'text-speak' and just be a line thought by Jane as she dresses sexily as previously instructed

by Matt. (Me: Um… Ok. Also, it's really cool that you notice this shit.)

10. Pg 143: Inserted 'Jesus.' in recalled text section so as to match original. Is this ok? (Me: Ok, but you do realize we don't recall thoughts/texts perfectly when we do recall them? We only recall the essentials.)

11. Pg 153: Recalled text line from Matt: earlier there is '…the sweet scent of you…,' not 'The sweet smell of you.' Amend 'smell' to 'scent'? (Me: Sure. I'm sure I meant to write scent both times. Smell has different connotations. Actually, I don't remember what I meant or why. Just use your judgement.)

12. Pg 157: Uses hyphen in ice cream. Consistent, so left as is. (Me: I hyphenated ice-cream? Really? Consistently? And you're not supposed to? Weird.)

13. Pg 194: Previous command by Matt was to start each request with 'Your whore says…' Is it ok to leave as 'Your whore begs…?' (Me: Yes! That was intentional. Um… what did you do in the copy edit? Do I need to go check?)

14. Pg 241: Beep as a sound, possibly put in italic? (Me: You really like sounds in italics, eh?)

15. Pg 254: Original comment from Jane's mother was that her father was going to look for a new place 'this week', not 'in a few days'. Replace? (Me: No. Because time passes. But if you did, I don't really care. Because, details. Boring.)

16. Pg 329: Query use of apostrophe, should this be completed by making into 'New Year's Day?' Or just leave as 'New Year?' (Me: Um… I dunno. Whatever you think is best?)

17. Pg 333: Phrase 'the evil bitch the universe' does not scan. Amended to 'the evil bitch of a universe' to fit in with other 'evil' universe-type comments by Jane. Is that ok? (Me: What does 'does not scan' mean?)

18. Pg. 340: UK readers may not realise this is referring to a skiing trip and the gondola refers to a ski-lift cable car gondola. Might it be worth considering amending to 'ski lift'

or 'cable car'? Just something to make the context more obvious. (Me: What the fuck is a cable car?)

19. Pg 476: Subtitle for Day 23 is Christmas Day – Tuesday, December 25. As a similar special day should Day 30 subtitle read as New Year's Day – Tuesday, January 1? (Me: You're really, really amazingly good at your job. Note to self: never, ever let anyone hire ME as a copy editor.)

The copy editor identifies the following words as 'dictionary' items (that is, I think, words not accepted by the house Dictionary):

- mindfuck
- bathtime
- cyberfuck
- dissing, speak disrespectfully to or criticize
- Eurotrash girl
- fuckslave
- jonesing, slang for addicted to something
- Netflix
- polyamory
- screenshot
- toke, to smoke a drug
- toque, type of brimless cap
- word-fuck

This all makes me ridiculous happy.

He flags these words as 'US English' (which is amusing to this Canadian), with the explanatory notes (to himself) in parentheses:

- coffeemaker
- Lavalife (CANADA an online dating service started in Toronto)
- makeup, same as UK English make-up
- parkade (CANADA multi-storey car park)
- *Penthouse Letters*, soft-porn magazine

- Timbits (CANADA brand name of a bite-sized confectionery sold at the Canadian-based franchise Tim Hortons)

There are also these miscellaneous notes:
- Montréal, but Montreal in text language is ok as special sorts not used in texting.
- Uses 'g-spot' in texting rather than 'G spot.' Consistent so left as is.
- Drink: green tea latte and green chai latte are same thing. (Are you sure?)
- Some hyphenation of terms ignored in sexting. Consistent. (Damn right, I'm consistent. Cause really, who hyphenates (or punctuates) when sexting?)

And this, clearly, is his favourite part:

Suggestion for blurb: section of sexting such as: I don't kiss you. I position you against me, and I slide my hands under your skirt. I shove the skirt up to your waist—and I'm very pleased you followed instructions, and there is a garter belt there, no panties. Very convenient for me.
—I obey.
You do.
And I reward.

EVERYONE ELSE, START READING AGAIN HERE:
But actually, the copy editor LOVES me.
Truth.
A. writes

[He's] is a hard man to please but says, "I liked this a lot. The writing is a cut above and the psychological insight a good deal sharper. Apart from some minor slips, it was a pretty straight run, copyediting wise. I didn't find anything that was ambiguous or confusing. I did (as

I mentioned in an earlier email) preserve the author's inconsistency of punctuation in these passages, and also allowed her to diverge from house style in matters like numbers (i.e. spelled-out vs. numerals), the presence of accents on French words, etc."

I feel so-very-special.

They are so going to let me keep all my cunts in the next book.

CONFESSION 26: *My parents still love me, although they'd love me more if I had written something they could show to their friends*

YOU ACTUALLY ASK this, remember?

So how do your parents feel about your new career as a pornographer?
—They're so proud.

It will, eventually, be the truth.
Right now, the truth is—my dad reads *Tell Me* accidentally—I mean, he reads it *on purpose*, I make it available to him *accidentally*.

Dad: It's fantastic! The dialogue! The relationships between the people! The sex... well, I skipped those parts.

Phew. Thank god. And if it's a lie, it's an important one.
My mom demands the manuscript of *Tell Me* as a Christmas present. Then she can't talk to or look at me for a few months.
She says a couple of things to me, right after, that... well, really, massively, hugely pissed me off.
She ends up reading *Tell Me* again a year or so later. "As if someone other than my daughter had written it," she says.

Which is the way you're supposed to read fiction, by the way. As FICTION. Not someone's dirty diary.

(I burn the pages of my dirty diary once a month. Any diarist who truly writes for herself, and not for posterity, should do the same.)

Anyway. On that second reading—she's somewhat less traumatized.

And proud. Or, at least, says she is. If it's a lie... it's an important one.

DRAFTS, DRAFTS & RE-DRAFTS:
I need a blurb but divorce is a buzz kill

DO YOU REMEMBER how I summarized *Tell Me* in my pitch to HarperCollins? It was accurate. It sold A.

But apparently, it's unmarketable.

A. writes:

I've been through your blurb again and think we should steer clear of mentioning divorce, marriages falling apart etc.; what's good about your book is that is realistically covers such ground, flawed expectations, impaired judgement etc., but it is very intense and sexy and authentic in tone. A kill-switch in romance/erotica is very often misery—this fiction is what they often read to escape that in their own lives. But once reading this, I think anyone who's been through a wringer will feed off the book and characters. But we have to get them there first. Also, safety catch on expletives like 'mindfuck.'

Do you want to have another stab at it? We could even use a choice line of dialogue that suggests the intensity but isn't too blue, and get that in the mix. At the mo' it's reading like a misery memoir. So, focus more on the passion, the risks, the intensity, the allure of an old flame, what's at stake. That's how we want to pitch this, as smoking hot, which it is, and not as a tear jerker, which it isn't. The humour is wonderful and a get out of jail card.

Sigh.

But ok.

He's the expert and the boss. And I can do this.

Take 1

"But you know what I want to know. Come on, Jane. This is me. Tell me. Tell me about..." her voice trails off.

She doesn't know exactly what it is she is asking for. But, of course, I know what it is she wants to hear.

She wants to hear you're my whore.
—She wants to hear that we fuck.
Do you think she could still look at you if she knew how?
—I expect so. That's not why I don't tell.
If you were going to tell her—what would you say?

What would I say? How do you explain twenty years of history, ten years of separation, and then, this insane desire that defies reason and shame—that is blind to risk? And how it's worth it, every moment of angst and fear because of the ecstasy it gives me? Would she understand? I don't know. I do not know what of this story is life's archetype and what is our own personal chemistry, own unique insanity.

Does it matter?
—Maybe not. What does matter?
Perfect trust, perfect understanding. The purity of our lust.
—Sophist.
Whore.
—Harlot.
Two of a kind.

Well, that's actually pretty good. I like it. Maybe a bit too long. Let's try it again.

Take 2

"Lover?"
"What, my bruised harlot?"
"Your flight boards in ten minutes."

"What? Oh, Jesus Christ. Give me my belt. Although I like it there, so very much."

"Pants first?"

"I suppose. Come here. Dress me. But... quickly."

"All right."

"Will you be all right? Dressing yourself, cleaning up?"

"Yes."

"Was I too rough?"

"Yes."

"I think I want you again."

"I see that. Eight minutes. Belt. Go."

"Going. Say thank you."

Thank you. Thank you, for what? For unhinging my sanity, threatening the stability of my life, with one text? Because that's how it begins, one text, one message. "I'm coming to town. Would like to see you." And I think... why not? Old friend. Oldest of friends. Favourite of ex-lovers. Married now, as am I. Both anchored in lives full of obligation, responsibility—to others. Safe. What's the harm? We're neither one of us stupid enough to risk our marriages, our families, our real lives.

Are we?

Does it matter?

—Maybe not. What does matter?

Perfect trust, perfect understanding. The purity of our lust.

—Sophist.

Whore.

—Harlot.

Two of a kind.

Getting there, right?

Take 3

But, Jane, and this is what you are asking: I am not looking for an out of my marriage. I am not looking to destroy yours. I am looking to fuck you senseless when I come. Use you. And leave.

Is that blunt and honest enough for you, my forever lover?

—Tell me you're not having a mid-life crisis, are not frustrated with your marriage, aren't ... oh, I don't even know what. What do I want you to tell me?

This: this is about us. Always. An opportunity. A gift. A chance to come together again.

And you want it as much as I do.

Do I? Do I? I am... I was happy. Stable marriage. Great kids. Friends. Family. Everything the way it was supposed to be. Everything fine. Everything... satisfactory. Maybe, a little boring?

Maybe. That's how it begins. I say maybe. And then—I totally lose control.

Now quickly. Tell me what you'll be doing in eight days, my lover.
—I'm afraid.
You will be on your fucking knees before me, my whore. Say it.
—Yes.
Good.

Final Version

A. and HarperCollins go with this:

Old flames burn brightest

This is about us. Always. An opportunity. A gift. A chance to come together again. And you want it as much as I do.

"Thank you for unhinging my sanity, threatening the stability of my life, with one text. Because that's how it begins, one text, one message. 'I'm coming to town. Would like to see you.'

And I think, why not? Old friend. Oldest of friends. Favourite of ex-lovers. Married now, as am I. Both anchored in lives full of obligation, responsibility to others. Safe. What's the harm? We're neither one of us stupid enough to risk our marriages, our families, our real lives. Are we?"

As Jane 'sexts' her lover and attempts to figure out how this aspect of herself fits into the obligations of marriage and motherhood, other relationships around her strain, fracture, and collapse.

Her best friend is recklessly pursuing a series of cyber-affairs, while another friend attempts an open, polyamorous marriage. Her next-door neighbour is planning a wedding with her on-again/off-again lover—but will it really happen?

Meanwhile her lawyer-husband is exchanging a lot of texts with an adoring young associate. Does Jane care? Or is she too engulfed in her own sanity-straining cyber affair to really notice?

I don't get marketing.
But.
Blurb!
Woo-hoo!

AN OBJECTION & A MYSTERY:
Leslie McIntyre on having it all

NOBODY OBJECTS TO a woman being a good writer or sculptor or geneticist if at the same time she manages to be a good wife, good mother, good looking, good tempered, well groomed, and unaggressive.

Leslie McIntyre

Mystery: Who the fuck is Leslie McIntyre? This quote appears in Julia Cameron's *The Artist's Way...* and since then has peopled the Internet. It is the only quotable thing Leslie McIntyre has ever said. Is she famous? Is she a she? Is she one of Cameron's students, friends? Is she an alias? *I need to know.* If you know, tell me. Please.

Also, homework: Today, take a moment and do your bit to combat the Madonna/Whore dichotomy. If you're a mother, 'fess up on one of your parenting forums that you kinda like looking at Internet porn. Some kinds, anyway. If you're a father, send the mother of your children a completely inappropriate text. While she's with your kids at toddler story time at the library. If you're a childless prude staring at me horrified, loosen up.

As an aside... have you ever noticed that there is no creature more uptight, prudish, and afraid of women's sexuality than the childless male? Call up a girlfriend and discuss...

CONFESSION 27:
I think this is what they mean by 'dialectics'

I'M VERY, VERY absorbed in *Tell Me* right now. So absorbed, hardly anything else matters.

—How difficult is it, really, to be married to me?
Him: As difficult, I suppose, as it is to be married to me.

But of course, other things are happening still. Marriage, children, love. Work-for-money, because, well, even if I had bothered to negotiate an advance, we would have eaten it long ago.

Good things. Bad things. Hard things. Portents of harder things.

Some things, I don't notice, because I'm so focused on *Tell Me*.

Some things, I don't want to notice. Because…

I don't want to talk about it, actually. Sorry.

Fucking again?
—Yeah. These are imperfect confessions, what can I say. I'm already telling you more than I planned.

But I'll tell you this: it's somewhere around here that I let M. Jane Colette fall in love. Not me. *Jane.*

It's incredible. Intoxicating. Insane.

She comes alive—becomes real.

120

The result is the beginning—or the middle, I'm not quite sure yet—of my third novel.

But I'm jumping ahead of the story. We still have to launch *Tell Me*.

(About the title of this Confession: I was going to define dialectics for you, also dialectical behaviour therapy, but instead, I'm going to send you to Google.)

FLASHBACK:
This part is totally true

TELL ME. WHAT does Matt look like? I need to know.

She texts me. It's 11 p.m., maybe later, and I'm in bed. I text back:

—What part are you on?
Her: Just finished Day 1.
—Ask me again when you get to Day 3.

And I turn off the phone and go to bed. (I don't see her "Good night, bitch!" message until the next morning.)
I give her a day before I reach out.

—Where are you now?
Her: Day 21. Reading now. Go away. Don't interrupt me.
—Do you still need to know what Matt looks like?
Her: Fuck, no. I don't care. Now go away. I'm READING!

Yeah.
That's what he looks like.
I smirk, a little full of myself.

CONFESSION 28:
A picture is worth a 1000 words

COVERS. WE ARE talking about covers.

So. This is A:

I'm wondering literal or abstract for the cover? I still get Desperate Housewives *from this and wonder if we should emulate that, or whether that show is current enough. I'll have a good think. If you see a cover you really like, send it over and I'll put it into the mix.*

This is me:

—It would be ridiculously important to me, if possible, that there be no people on the cover. Have you noticed? Nobody is ever described. And yet every woman who's read the book 'knows' what Matt looks like. It's awesome. I don't want to spoil it. On the photo shoot we did for the m jane colette site, for the photos I'm using on there, we did a bunch of shots of the phone, of Jane texting etc. I'm attaching a few for you... I know it's not traditional erotica-cover sexy... but. *Tell Me*'s not traditional erotica, either.

—I don't think any of the shots work as a cover shot, but just an idea of where my head is with it.

He hates all my ideas. Well, not exactly. But he says:

...technology on a cover is a hard sell. Let me think on it.

But I keep on trying.

—I'm attaching the two images that to me personally came closest to capturing what the book's about, but they centre on that damn phone. (Which is the centrepiece in another piece I'm writing right now, "How texting ruins everything." But that's entirely off-topic.) I think the phone in beautiful hands, over the curve of sexy legs… that would be very evocative.

—We all live our love affairs (divorces, too) through phones right now…

—For me, the whole "Tell me" "I don't tell" thing is THE defining tone of the book. How does one convey it? A stylized face, lips covered? Phone against lips? Man's hand over mouth—but that becomes cheesy and non-consensual…

—This is really hard. I'm so much more about the words than the pictures…

—Other ideas—this next bit, these are all suggestions from my beta readers, who've chosen to hyper-focus on the weirdest things (I'm omitting all the handcuffs references because there are no fucking handcuffs or blindfolds or stupid props in the book!):

- "dress and fuck-me heels thrown on bed"
- "stockings or tie/belt draped over laptop"
- "boot shot—those sexy boots she gets from Matt at the end, but surrounded by children's toys or little sandals or something?" (I don't know about this one)
- "a play on the boots and the minivan—maybe her leg in a boot or the heels she wears to the airport, stepping out of that Mommy van?"
- "single flower, an orchid. In a vase, knocked over? Flowers are sexy" (Me: There are no flowers in the book. *Her: There's that line: 'Do you want me to bring you flowers, fuckslave?'*)

124

- "I'm thinking something evocative but fuzzy. Like one small detail is in focus but everything else is not. Like the knee high boots off the end of a bed and a blurry body in the background?"
- "a simple texting screen with title and details in texts"
- "all family boots in the hall—business shoes, kids shoes, and those sexed up dominatrix boots she gets" (Me: They're not dominatrix boots! *Her: They're totally dominatrix boots. Six inch heels and buckles.* [I never, ever describe them.])
- "lingerie on stairs or floor"
- "shot of woman's shoulder/chest showing only lingerie under her coat? Can that be done tastefully?"
- "the belt. Man's belt, on bed? Or in woman's hands?" (this is kind of interesting…)

—I wish my favourite photographer hadn't screwed off for Cuba this week so I could play with a couple of these and send you roughs.

—Anyway. Hopefully something sparks you and your artists? I must now return to my lower calling of spinning lies for Corporate Canada.

A. writes:

Some interesting ideas here—I can almost see the covers. I'll put some of these into the cover brief and have a good look online myself and see if we can distil some of the book's spirit. The main thing with this readership is not looking porno, or sleazy, or hard BDSM, and instead appearing sophisticated but sexy. Too great an emphasis on heels can denote female domination, though that depends on how its done, but a single iconic image of a heeled shoe or boot is a signifier of female sexual power—I'd say this book is a battle between empowerment and capitulation to herself. Legs in stockings I love with everything, but it's the female eye we have to target. I still wonder about

abstract—we can't rule it out. A bed may be interesting, and we could
include a phone on it. Anyway, leave it with me.

    I do.
And he does great.
The cover we end up with, I LOVE.
How about you?

By the way, did you catch this?

I'd say this book is a battle between empowerment and capitulation
to herself.

I LOVE HIM.
He got every single fucking nuance.

A CLARIFICATION:
She's a fuckslave, he likes to be called master, but I do not write stereotypical BDSM scenes with blindfolds and handcuffs, thank you very much

THERE ARE NO handcuffs, whips, blindfolds, no lame-ass (sorry if that's your kink, it's not Jane's) props of any sort in *Tell Me*.

Twice, they banter about Matt's belt. But that's it.

Why do all my readers keep on feeding me bondage images?

I think it's the thirty-seven occurrences of 'fuckslave' in the text.

—You know, I still don't get it. Fuckslave, a-ok. Cunt—a no go.

Move on.

—I am, I have.

I totally haven't.

Two years later, I still miss every single one of my cut cunts.

CONFESSION 29:
I will never forget...

...THE WAY WE celebrated my FIRST cover.
My. First. Cover.
My. Book.
So high.
We celebrate.
Do you remember?
<3

CONFESSION 30: *The way to hell is paved with the best intentions*

ANTICIPATION, SWELLING OF…

I have a meeting with my beta readers aka my street team—although I don't learn that term for another year—to plan marketing activities around the book launch. The meeting includes two savvy yyc PR mavens.

Them: So what we need to know, really, is what HarperCollins is going to do for you so that we can work with it and build on it.
—Um. I don't know. They haven't really said.
Them: Can you ask them?

I can. I do. They don't really say.

I want to be clear here: the problem is mutual. I'm so green, I don't even know what questions to ask. My editor-contact is overworked and overwhelmed. The publisher is digesting the acquisition of Harlequin… and struggling with some pretty massive 'Who are we supposed to be in this Brave New World of Publishing, E-Content, Free E-Books, Too Many Authors Not Enough Readers' challenges.

I'm not important in their big picture.

That's fine.

My girls got my back.

We make plans.

We none of us really know how to market an e-book— and I'm not clear on how the print part of my release will work. The title will be available in print-on-demand, I'm told—but no one ever explains to me how that will work.

Here's an example of a typical communication exchange between me and my publishers:

—Any word on print-on-demand?

A: Will look again. It should have happened now. I have Tell Me *as a priority title.*

—Ok, keep me posted…

Clear as mud?

Yeah.

All of this uncertainty makes it difficult to plan. I have no print books, and I don't know how to, for example, do a virtual launch party. I don't want to do a physical real-world launch party without a guarantee that a physical book will be available for it.

Also—I can't do a physical launch party because, um, M. Jane Colette, who's M. Jane Colette?

I don't know—all I know is I don't want people to know she's me.

You're self-conscious about those four unexpurgated cunts.

—No… Maybe? I don't know.

Let me own this, completely, now, even before we get to Launch Day:

I thoroughly fuck up my launch and fail to capitalize on the momentum of the new release for two reasons.

1. I don't know what the fuck I'm doing.
2. I'm not owning being M. Jane Colette. She may have a headshot and a website now… but she's still not real. She's not me. I don't want people to know she's me.

There's also this: all my *Right-Brain Business Plan* visioning work notwithstanding, I don't want to have to 'sell' the book. I wrote it. I placed it with a publisher.

Isn't it their job to sell it?

QUESTION: *Isn't it their job to sell it?*

ANSWER: NO, APPARENTLY not.

(Also, do you remember... in my exercises for my business plan, when I wrote:

I want to give Tell Me *the best possible shot to be found, read, and enjoyed. I don't want to be passive about its success—I don't want to rely on the publisher deciding to put effort into it. I want to do everything I can to make it fly.*

I lied. I want the publisher to do everything. Or at least something. Because I still don't know what to do.)

CONFESSION 31:
Instead of really preparing myself for the launch, I wrap myself in Persian Poetry

I WILL NOT deny what I desire.
My lips want your lips,
not a substitute.

Hafez

—Oh, fuck, yes!
Him: He's talking about Allah, God, the Divine, you know, you heathen whore.
—He. Is. Not.
Him: He is.

I don't care. I wrap myself in the words, drown myself in them. Oh, fuck. I think I just touched the Divine. What a nasty trick to play on an atheist, Sufi mystic.
Words.

Your Hafez reader:
If you need to be coaxed into poetry, start with Daniel Ladinsky's *The Gift: Poems by Hafiz, the Great Sufi Master*. These aren't actually 'true' Hafez poems —they're not even attempts at translation. They're more like riffs on the Persian poet by an enamoured American poet. But they are still beautiful.

133

This is the best Hafez translation I have found: *Faces of Love: Hafez and the Poets of Shiraz* by Dick Davis.

This one is almost as good: *The Tangled Braid: Ninety-Nine Poems by Hafiz of Shiraz*, translated by Jeffrey Einboden and John Slater.

And if you just want to dip your toe into the ocean of Persian (and other) poetry gently, start with the Hafez page on poetry-chaikhana.com.

CONFESSION 32:
The book's coming out tomorrow, and I am going mad

I TEXT *HER*, because I've texted you three times in the last hour, and I feel I ought to spread the crazy, just a little, you know? So I text her, and she asks the right question, and I say:

—Oscillating between pumped-ecstatic and fucking terrified.

And then she holds my hand for a while, all via text:

Her: Terrified of?
—Failure.
Her: Ah. Always possible, but highly unlikely. It is a truly brilliantly written book. It is a voice unlike any I've never read. I think the unintentional (;-P) psychological exploration of fidelity is nuanced and subtle. If it flops, it will just make me think less of humanity than I already do…

And I love her, oh, I love her, would you not? My bruised-frightened-battered-ego preens, for a moment. But, reality:

—It has a lot of crappy competition to cut thru…

135

Her: Yup. That will be the hard part. You'll have stealth on your side as it can pass for just erotica for those who don't get the more intelligent stuff but I think once it gets picked up by a smarty or two it will get lots of word of mouth.

Word of mouth. Right. Word of mouth. Words on a screen...

Promotion. Marketing. Ugh. My stomach turns. I. So. Don't. Want. To. And she knows. They all know. They're supposed to do it for me, because that's what friends and beta readers do, right?

Her: I'm actually feeling a bit funny about the desire to promote you to my friends but also to maintain your anonymity. Not sure how to work that...

—'I know this writer...'

Her: Yeah but I already gushed about it when I read it!

—Well, they won't remember who you were gushing about.

Her: I'm worried I'm not subtle enough. I'm a shitty liar. I'm thinking ... accidentally leaving copies of it places.

—Lol. Expensive.

Her: Like Dr. Offices. How embarrassing would that be, to start reading right before an internal exam? Oh, uh, it's not you, doctor, I was just thinking about Matt and Jane....

This is an actual true story. You can tell, because the cadence of reality is clunky. Also, I have the screen shots to prove it.

I also have the most amazing support network.

Which loves me at my whiniest, whiniest, lowest worst.

Which reminds me—I have an exercise from the depths of despair for you.

When you think you're alone, unsupported, an island— get out a piece of paper and a pen (you can type if you need to, but it really does work better longhand) and start making a list of all the people who've got your back, who you can call when you need help.

You can stop when you fill both sides of the paper and start looking for page three.

If you can't fill both sides of the paper—you gotta start building your support network, baby.

But that's the topic of someone else's book.

Let's go back to my book now, shall we? The one with too many pussies, and hardly any cunts.

It comes out... tomorrow.

Are you ready?

I'm not.

CONFESSION 33: *I am a writer. Today, finally, I am a REAL writer...*

MAY 28, 2015.

This is a really awesome day.

My beta readers are amazing, and they all start buying the book as soon as it's available for sale—which means that on May 28, and for a few days after, *Tell Me* climbs beautifully through the erotica e-book ranks, hitting and holding the #3 spot on Amazon.

(In reality, by the way, I find out later that this is not the result of several thousand or several hundred sales but more like several dozen. Sob. But I don't know it then, and #3 feels pretty fucking awesome).

I am high. I am happy. I. Am. An. Author.

True thing: I have been writing all my life, publishing and getting paid for my writing since I was seventeen—and supporting my family with my writing for the past decade and a half.

It is only in this moment, with a published *novel* to show for it, that I feel I'm a real writer. What's that about?

A misspent childhood.
—What?
A childhood spent reading too many novels.

Maybe. Doesn't matter.

Today, I am an author. I. Am. An. Author. Squee.

THIS REALLY HAPPENS:
How do you criticize someone's sexual fantasies, exactly?

I DON'T SEE this one coming.

She wants me to teach her how to write erotica, and she sends me something she's written. And then, texts me while I'm reading it.

Her: Well? What do you think?

I'm still reading, and what I'm thinking, at this moment, is that the immediacy of texting has wrecked people. I have not had time to read what she wrote, let alone react to it. But she is waiting for a response.

And don't think I'm judging or condemning her—I am the same. When I text you and don't hear back from you for an hour, I am certain you no longer love me.

Anyway.

I'm still reading.

She's impatient.

Her: It's the pacing, isn't it. The pacing's all the wrong. It's too fast.

It's not. The pacing's fine. But there is something... wrong with what she wrote. For me, anyway. But how do I tell her?

Critiquing someone else's sexual fantasies is sort of like...

Ok, I can't think of an adequate comparison...

Here's what I say (text) instead:

—So, for me, for erotica to work—for sexual fantasy to work—it has to be something that actually could happen. You know what I mean?

Her: But isn't the whole point of fantasy that you get to live out, in your head, something you can't have in real life?

—Sort of. Otherwise we'd all be documentarians, not fiction writers. But see, all the BEST fiction works because on some basic level... it feels real. I don't care if you're writing about unicorns, aliens, or zombies—the more outrageous the unreal elements, the more critical it is that the story be true. That it feel like it could happen.

Her: So... what I wrote—you don't think it could happen?

—I don't believe it. It doesn't feel real.

Her: Why?

Ha. If only I knew...

And if only I knew how to tell her without breaking her artist's heart...

I don't know what to say.

So I lie.

—Perhaps because I know you so well. But it's beautifully, beautifully written.

It's a white lie, and like all white lies should be, kind and necessary.

CONFESSION 34:
Squirming with embarrassment, and not at what you might think...

REMEMBER, YOU ASKED how my parents felt about me being a pornographer?

I think that was the wrong question.

My dad writes this review of *Tell Me:*

Tell me, it is impossible! Marushka spilled the milk again (Master and Margaret) *and things started to roll. Contemporary Colette is alive and kicking* Grey's *ass! Sorry, E.L. James, you will have to change his name to Dorian!*

It did not take this Emmanuelle 9 1/2 weeks *to turn hers and her friends' lives upside down. The* Nymphomaniac-*like narrative is very engulfing and deeply hypnotic. It is truly Lars Von Trier's screenplay material!* Tell Me *is projecting its images on the screen of your mind. I could not put it aside, I could not wait for the images to play in my brain again. And I was truly, deeply disappointed when it ended.*

To be perfectly clear—there were at least two different universes I've experienced while under the influence of this read. All of them mind-boggling and actually quite disturbing. These were all conceived by the mind of a woman (I presume) who writes like a man (I think) and has mastered an understanding of men and their secret desires. Cannot wait for the sequel. And where the heck is Calgary? Have to go and see it by myself!

I don't let him post it.

But I accept its creation and existence as an immense gift of love.

My mom is still navigating. And—like me—she doesn't quite know how to show me support without outing me as... well, a pornographer, to use your term. She shares the link to *Tell Me*'s Amazon listing on her Facebook. "Interesting read," she says demurely.

My dad jumps in: "She hasn't been the same since she's read it!"

Ugh.

Much as my cunt-lite but still chockfull of cocks, whores, clits, fuckslaves, and cum narrative may have mildly traumatized my parents, the fact that they've read it has, to be frank, mildly traumatized me.

An Interlude For An Orgasm

THINGS ARE ABOUT to get kind of dark and yucky, so before they do, let's slip into a warm bath and have an orgasm or two. Ok?

So.
Bath.
The sexy thing about visualizing a lover in a bath is the intersection of exposed and covered. Naked, but submerged. The water covers and reveals. Distorts, teases, invites.

Your breasts are not submerged, and so, if I were there, sitting on the edge of that bath tub, I would see them. And want to touch them, want to find out if I could find evidence of the piercing in the right one? Could I? Could I see it with my eyes, feel it with my fingers? My tongue?

Tongue on, and then lips, and, of course, teeth. Nip. And then, look up. Was that ok? Allowed? No censure, no slap. Maybe, the hint of a moan. Nip. Lick. A full-face caress.

And because I always want what I cannot have, I look at that left one. The unbiteable one. Unreclaimed. Yours, and so, in no part mine. I trace around it with a finger. Then with my nose, cheek, mouth—explore all around the breast, but never near the nipple.

Then—to the right. Nip. Hard. And now, a moan, a reaction. Yes. Finally.

One of the most erotic experiences of my life: my arms above my head, bound to a hotel headboard with a scarf. My scarf. A breath on my nipples. First on this one, then on the other. Lips brushing, but never touching. A flicker of a tongue. Hands under, beside, over, but never on. I am driven mad, I am insane: I need that tongue, those lips, I need them chewing on my nipples, I. Need. Them.

"Suck," I whisper. "Oh, for fuck's sake. Suck!"

"Beg," the voice, hot, ragged, busy breathing, teasing. "Beg."

I would. I want to. I want nothing more. But I am so mad, so mad, I cannot form the words. Never was a 'p' more clumsy. Never did an 'l' take so much effort.

Finally: "Pleeeez…"

I cum before the teeth touch me. Anticipation.

The hardness of the nipple, the softness of the breast. It is the most erotic combination; the only other body part that comes close is… the thigh. Cunt lips? Delicious and fascinating, of course, but there is something about the thigh…

I learn about the allure of thighs from someone else, in a text. "Today, I am all about the thigh. That is all I see. Every woman—she is thighs, two thighs, a body above and bones and flesh below… thighs. I would grasp each, fervently, and lose myself within them," he writes.

"Between them?" I ask.

"Within them. It's not… well, of course, ultimately, I suppose it is about what's between them. But today, right now, I don't need their cunts. I just want the thighs. They are… everything. Promise incarnate. Soft… yet so fucking sturdy. They need to carry all of each of you. And when they spread for me? Or are forced open? No other feeling compares."

So. The next time I am with a woman's thighs… I explore. I pretend the cunt isn't there. I don't touch, I don't look, I don't smell. Just the thighs. I trace. Knead... lick. Kiss. Look so very closely. Nip very gently. Bite.

Never come close to her cunt, never even graze her clit, tease a lip, approach a hole. Don't cross the line towards the curve of the ass.

Just about the thigh.

She explodes and gushes me, rivers, rivulets of lust and desire, soaking her thighs, and my exploring hands.

It can be all about the thigh.

Yours are under the water, and water interferes with touch; it is its own element and experience, and it dislikes competition. The water ripples, and all is distorted, except the triangle—or is it a line?—of dark pubic hair. I want to yank it, hard, just so you yell no, and slap me, and yank mine.

Instead, I press, deliberately, on your button of a clit. And then move my hand away, and rest it on a sunken thigh.

I speak with my thighs, I know this, they respond to touch and word. And when they spread, when I open, I am wantonness defined. They don't just invite. They beg.

"Come. Cum."

When I am done—sated, exhausted, satisfied—I pull them closed, tight. Roll on my side, tuck knees almost to chin. Done, done... but, when they are forced apart at that moment, oh fuck yes, wanton again, and that is when I cum the hardest.

I don't know the language or geography of your thighs yet.

So many things to learn.

CONFESSION 35:
And then, everything falls apart

I'M NOT GOING to tell you about this part.

This part, still, is for my eyes only.

I guess what you need to know, for the story to make sense, is that awful, awful things happen in the middle of the happiest most amazing things.

So, an awful thing happens.

Call it another truck—I should be consistent with my metaphors, no?

Another truck. And… and I can't pay attention to *Tell Me*. At all. I need to keep my family, my life together, and there's no space in my head for chasing influencers, asking for book reviews, building a Twitter following, arranging readings, joining fora, blog tours… there is no space in my head for anything, but holding things together.

Pause

"BUT…"
    "SHUSH."
    "BUT…"
    "Shut up. Ssshhh. Just… be… silent."
It's very difficult.
But I do it.

A CONSULTATION WITH
THOMAS WOLFE:
But surely there's a purpose to all this

...GOD IS NOT always in his Heaven, all is not always right with the world. It is not all bad, but it is not all good, it is not all ugly, but it is not all beautiful, it is life, life, life—the only thing that matters. It is savage, cruel, kind, noble, passionate, selfish, generous, stupid, ugly, beautiful, painful, joyous—it is all these, and more, and it's all these I want to know ... and I will put it on paper, and make it true and beautiful.

...

When I speak of beauty I do not mean a movie close-up where Susie and Johnnie meet at the end and clinch and all the gum-chewing ladies go home thinking husband is not so good a lover as Valentino. That's cheap and vulgar. I mean everything which is lovely, and noble, and true. It does not have to be sweet, it may be bitter, it does not have to be joyous, it may be sad.

Thomas Wolfe, *Letters To His Mother*

CONFESSION 36:
Wait, I lied

THERE'S NO SPACE in my head for anything... except...

... um...

I take two marathon weekends... and I...

... do you know what I do?

I write another book.

Holy fuck.

I do.

I really do.

So, I'm oversimplifying a little—for the sake of an effective narrative. Deal with it—I'm a writer, and you're here with me, after all, because of my super-power to mould reality into *story*.

In this version of the story, the chronology goes like this: *Tell Me* is published. Everything comes apart. I write another book to deal with it.

Neat, simple.

Party true.

A slightly closer-to-reality chronology goes like this: I finish writing *Tell Me* in June 2013. I get hit by a truck. I sleepwalk through life for four months—wake up, very briefly, at a Christmas party with this idea. Could I? Could I write a love story, a romance, the happy ending in which is a divorce, and where the central relationships are all the non-romantic relationships between women, because... no, wait, up the stakes a little, could I write it in such a way that it was the resolution of *those* relationships that kept the reader turning the pages… but the whole thing still worked, also, as a modern romance?

I think I could… I see the potential story arc—the characters—the relationships among them… I sketch them out on a piece of paper I pull out of the Christmas party host's recycling.

My fog and stupidity return quickly thereafter, and all that happens to the idea is that I come up with a working title for it—*Methadone*—and I carry that paper around with me everywhere I go.

But I don't write a word.

Until—do you remember? I fall in the love by the river and decide to stop being completely, totally crazy… and I meet an artist who mixes magic potions in her studio… and somewhere, between the magic spun by those two magicians—the woman I fall in love with, she tells me, do you remember, she says,

You HAVE the chops to do it.

…and I believe her, if only for a minute, if only because those words are coming out of lips I want to kiss—the artist says, does nothing—she doesn't care about me, at all, all she cares about it her work, her canvasses, her art, and that is the most intoxicating thing I have ever seen—somewhere in that moment, I wake up.

Awake, I start to write.

But… actually, if we are really telling the truth—and right now, I feel I owe you the truth, because of my earlier evasions and obfuscations—one more thing has to happen. I have to send *Tell Me* out into the world—and I do, I prepare and write those pitches and send them to HarperCollins *et al*. And then, I take out my slip of paper and stare at it.

And despair again.

I have no idea how to begin.

The first novel was a fluke.

I am an idiot. An impostor. A one-hit wonder, and I haven't actually even had that one hit yet, I just...

Sob.

She tries, one more time.

Her: Have you read Julia Cameron's The Artist's Way*?*

—Sounds fucking pretentious. Anyway, I'm no artist.

Her: You might find it helpful. Right now. Or, you know. You can just stay bat-shit crazy and unproductive forever.

—Fuck you. I'm working. I'm doing all the things I have to do.

Her: Well. But you're not writing. Anyway. Just a suggestion.

I read Julia Cameron's *The Artist's Way*. It's hokey and pretentious, and writing Morning Pages, as the answer to all of life's ills, really?

Says Julia:

Morning Pages are three pages of longhand, stream of consciousness writing, done first thing in the morning. **There is no wrong way to do Morning Pages—they are not high art**. *They are not even 'writing.' They are about anything and everything that crosses your mind—and they are for your eyes only. Morning Pages provoke, clarify, comfort, cajole, prioritize, and synchronize the day at hand. Do not over-think Morning Pages: just put three pages of anything on the page...and then do three more pages tomorrow.*

I burned all my journals when I was eighteen, and I am not going to start journaling again. It's a narcissistic, destructive-not-creative practice. Screw you, Julia. Not gonna do it.

Her: Sarah Selecky's writing prompts.

—What?

Her: Check it out. Sarah Selecky's writing prompts. On SarahSelecky.com.

She tells me about this resource perhaps six times before I hear her. I'm not writing. But I'm awake. I ought to be writing. I need to be writing. I want to be writing.

I'm still a little broken, a little mad. I need help.

Her: Sarah...
—Ok, ok!

I sign up. Every morning, there's a writing prompt in my email in-box.

And I start writing. Every morning. First for ten minutes. Twenty. Thirty. An hour.

Over July and August 2014, every morning, by hand—that's how I write the first draft of the novel I'm then still calling *Methadone.*

Well, first draft is a bit of a grandiose term for what I create.

What I actually do: each morning, Sarah Selecky emails me a writing prompt. And I use that writing prompt to write... about Elizabeth. Annie. Zia. Sasha. The men they love (and don't).

Without sense of plot, purpose, structure. Scene upon scene, vignette upon vignette.

Half-way through that exercise, HarperCollins offers on *Tell Me*—and I get an incredible boost, and start seeing *Methadone* not as therapy (it sort of feels like therapy for the first little while) but a work in progress.

One day, in early September, I hit a point at which I start to think I'm done. I mean—that in the three or four notebooks I've filled at that point, I have a complete first draft of a novel.

This happens: I put it away, don't look it, don't think about it for the next six months.

In March 2015, I type it up. Put the separate scenes on dozens and dozens of index cards.

Only see its flaws, holes, imperfections.

Hate. It. HATE IT.

Tell Me is published. Everything falls apart. I bring *Methadone* to a close in two weekends not because I want to, but because I have to. I. Have. To. Finish. It. That urgency comes from… where? My personal crisis? The need to prove that *Tell Me* is not a one-off? The fear that I am running out of time—that I only have this week, this weekend, to do, start, finish anything?

I don't know.

I finish it, in two weekends.

Spend another month caressing it, polishing it, preparing it for beta readers.

Retitle it *Defensive Adultery*.

Retitle it *Consequences*.

Send it to the beta readers as *The Book Formerly Known as Methadone, Now Probably Consequences—unless you like Defensive Adultery Better?*

Here. Want a tiny taste? I'm going to throw you into the middle of a conversation, between Elizabeth and her lover.

…to be frank, there was a rather prolonged period in my life when I thought adultery was hot. And I miss your wedding ring, a little.

—That's because you're a psychopath.

I'm an artist with mildly sociopathic tendencies and a lack of comfort with dominant social mores. But enough about me. This is your story.

My story. Her story. The new story. There's no space in my head, my life that summer for *Tell Me*. I tell myself it's because… because of what I am holding together.

But maybe… maybe it was because of *Consequences*.

(Or, do you like *Defensive Adultery* better? Tell me. There's still time to change it…)

153

LESSON: *He had a teenie weenie penis, and that's why you should read Anne Lamott*

THERE ARE ALL sorts of good reasons to read Anne Lamott's *Bird By Bird*, and if you are interested in having these explained to you, read "Writing And How Perfectionism Kills Creativity" or "9 Books On Reading and Writing," both on BrainPickings.org, the best place on the Internet for lovers of words, writers, books, and angst.

The most important reason to read Anne Lamott's *Bird By Bird*, however, is this:

Libel is defamation by written or printed word. It is knowingly, maliciously saying things about people that cast them in a false or damaging light. That means that if you lived with a man who had a number of curious personal and professional habits and circumstances that his friends and clients happen to know about, and if these friends can identify this man in your work by these habits and circumstances, you should probably change the details dramatically...However, if he revealed himself...to be a sociopathic narcissist, you can attempt to capture his character and use actual descriptions, just as long as this specific man is not identified by your descriptions. ...Make yourself the first wife or the girlfriend, instead of the third wife, and do not include his offensive children, especially the red-haired twins...And the best advice I can give you is to give him a teenie little penis so he will be less likely to come forth.

I'm so glad someone put it down in black and white.

CONFESSION 37:
I'd really like someone to blame, but...

I SEND *CONSEQUENCES* (we could still call it *Defensive Adultery*—we really need to talk about this) to A. on August 10, 2015.

The cover letter is neither an introduction nor a pitch. It is all... tease...

*

What's that?
—This? Nothing. A photograph.

He looks at the photograph, and demands a story I don't want to tell.

Isn't this what all women want? A lover who's passionately interested in the quotidian details of their excruciatingly boring, dysfunctional lives—as well as skilled with hands, and tongue, and cock?

No. Not me. Or do I? I start to talk. I tell him about... about all of them. And, inadvertently, me. Things I've never put into words for anyone before...

That's the game you and I are playing. Do you not know that? I am looking for the key. And you're trying not to give it to me. But you want to play, and so you keep on talking, and so eventually, you will.

I'm very careful not to say too much. I sure as hell am not going to take my somewhat sociopathic lover of the moment into the tragedy of my life.

Why not? Tragedy is erotic. The things that make you laugh don't make you hard. Or wet, lover, as the case may be. Check yourself.

Fuck. Really? I'm doing this? Why?

Because you want to. Because you're compelled. Does it matter? Just talk.

So. I do.

*

A. writes back:

Consider me teased.

Good. That's done.
Tell Me… Tell Me I don't pay attention to, at all. Nominally, it's because my beta readers and I agree, way back when, to wait for the big launch until we have print copies to play with. My deal for the book, if you recall, was for e-books and print-on-demand—which means, no print copies in stores, but paperbacks available for order and sale online. But even back in August 2014, that seemed to me to be, so very clearly, the future of all book publishing (bar that one per cent defined by J. K. Rowling *et al.*), I didn't worry about it. Print-on-demand sounded just fine. Happy to sign off on that.

Except, um… one, two, three, four, five months later—the only way you can get *Tell Me* is... as an e-book.

Which is fine, actually. Fine.

I'm fine to wait. I poke the publisher every once in a while, but honestly, at some level—I'm happy to wait until we have the print-on-demand sorted out. Because, until that happens… all I have to do is… wait.

It's convenient.

Because, you see—in September, October 2015—a published author for an entire quarter now!—I still have no idea how to sell a book.

Not a clue.

And…

I confess…

…I don't want to learn how to do it. At all.

I'd rather memorize poems by Hafez and…

…trace his profile with my fingers, eyes, and tongue…

…and chase sweet smoke with you in a sheesha lounge…

…and day dream about a winter in Cuba…

Oooh. I should go to Cuba for the winter. Mmm. I totally should. I hate winter. I love Cuba.

I love you.

I hate marketing. Sales. Promotion.

I hate *Tell Me*.

It's a terrible book, and I should have never written it. Also, *Consequences*. What the fuck was I thinking? That is not how a book is written, structured, presented.

I'm an idiot.

An impostor.

Loser.

Deluded.

I should get a real job. Go back to corporate whoring.

I whore a little. Cash the cheques.

Buy tickets for me and my kids to go to Cuba.

PLEASE PASS THE CHAMPAGNE:
He loves me! He loves me again!

ON SEPTEMBER 29, 2015, there's an email from A. in my inbox that makes life worth living again:

I hope this finds you well. Sorry for the delay, but I can only offer all of the usual valid reasons (running this on my own being chief). Anyway, I have read and enjoyed Consequences. *It's as special as* Tell Me, *in its own way. You might even be a subgenre to yourself.*

Some more thoughts as I went along:

They're strange things, your books. I find them compelling but they also leave me slightly aghast. It's the cognitively overloaded lifestyles of the people, their myriad issues, the respective senses of entitlement, the resentment and hostility they nurture, the explosive, near feral sex used like a drug that is part of, and yet fuels, the root manias.

They're very interesting stories but a hard fit in the genre of wishful thinking that is ER, because they take on reality, even if they make it larger than life in a slightly mad, hyper-real, even grotesque way that no one would covet (but that good fiction should pursue). They kind of force a voyeurism, but limit empathy with any character. Compulsive slightly toxic people instigating explosions. But I do find the books stimulating and vivid and authentic though; you're kind of straddling general fiction with some literary overtones, and they're almost screenplays of dysfunctional lives behind the middle class, like American Beauty *was.*

As a kind of subtext I think you're identifying a cultural trend of lives full of intense feeling that lack self-awareness or empathy (some might say a near sociopathic behaviour created by the consequences of unregulated capitalism and the inequality and competitiveness it produces). Everyone is an addict save the slightly dim, accepting husbands. There are no princes or Cinderellas so they are a hard fit in romance. I think this is why most women read romance: to escape this world. But I think all romance should have an element of this in it, though, but then I'm not a woman, or the core readership. But I suspect a few Zias are the core readers (from what I have seen at conventions).

Isn't it a shame that popular fiction is like this now. Horror is the same; if it matters and has some poignant meaning, and is well-written, you are suddenly confronted by the realisation that most readers of the books have the minds of eleven-year-olds that play computer games all night, and will hate the 'sophistication' and complexity. And publishing just follows the money.

On structure you're being innovative, which I enjoy, and most readers should be able to pick up the untraditional structure of the narrative—a dialogue over memory. It's like watching a film with the commentary track on.

But, I really like it and your books offer something different. I say that so much now that I fear half of the list is left field and alternative. So, even though this isn't romance, or strictly erotica (though there is erotica in this and it's filthy), I can offer the same terms as the last book, if you're game.

And I am told the POD situation will be sorted out soon too. I have Tell Me *as a priority title.*

I am amazing.

I. Am. An. Author.

A real fucking author, with two fucking books written. TWO. BOOKS.

ME.

I am amazing.

I'm also a little more experienced now.

159

My first book may have been published by Harper-fucking-Collins (which is still a wow factor for me), but Harper-fucking-Collins didn't really do anything to help promote me, and... well... where the fuck are the print copies? I mean, Amazon's CreateSpace churns them out within forty-eight hours. This should not be taking six months.

So.

I... demure:

—...although arrogantly fairly confident the book was good, I also knew it was neither romance nor erotica and so didn't really think you'd be interested. Thrilled that you are, and your commentary was... well. It pleased.

—Do you mind if I hold off on making a decision until I see that the POD situation is sorted out? I'm old enough that I need print books... and I still haven't had my *Tell Me* launch party, because I want to have print copies at it... and if I never see a print copy of my second novel, my cold heart will break.

—Also—all the occurrences of the word 'cunt' in this book are kinda important. Would I get to keep them?

Again with the cunts?

—It's fucking important.

A. understands. Will keep me updated on POD—will let me take my time.

And... wait for it... he says I'd get to keep my cunts this time.

Ha.

Good.

Still.

I'm going to wait.

And that's where we leave it.

And, I—I fuck off to Cuba.

Before you go...

—Yes, my darling?

Who the fuck is Zia? You know? When A. says "Zias are the core readers" of romance and erotica?

—Zia is one of the characters in *Consequences*. An ex-wife with arrested development. Yes, if she were a dude, she'd have a teenie weenie penis. As it is, she spends a lot of time worrying about her Botox injections.

You're not fond of her then.

—She is occasionally the villain of the piece. Except when she's its victim.

CONFESSION 38:
I fuck off to Cuba and write another book

I GO TO Cuba to… but that's another story, and some of it is told in the #postcardsfromcuba project on my alter-ego's blog, NothingByTheBook.com, if you're interested.

What's important for this story is that… I arrive in Cuba with two corpses inside me.

What?
—It's a metaphor and I'm getting to the explanation…
I'm starting to distrust your boast that you know how to craft a narrative.
—I'm letting you see how my mind and process works. It is not exactly linear.
Understatement of the decade.
—Are you going to shut up and let me get back to telling the story?
Please. Cuba. Two corpses. Lovely image. Continue.

Two corpses. I'm a writer, so you know what I'm talking about. Not *Tell Me* or *Consequences* (but do you think… *Defensive Adultery*? There are lots of books out there called *Consequences*. I don't think there's one called *Defensive Adultery*). *Tell Me* and *Consequences* are alive and kicking.

The corpses... The corpses have a long backstory. Let me attempt to summarize: at some point over the summer during which everything was falling apart and I was writing *Consequences* while not marketing *Tell Me*, I started thinking about a memoir-type project. It was going to be about that getting hit by a truck incident of June 2013 and its consequences and everything falling apart, maybe.

True thing: when you turn suffering into art, it becomes bearable. More—noble.

Almost... beautiful.

I was going to call it *Catalyst*. And it was going to completely revolutionize the way people think about unconditional love.

—Don't say it. Delusional, I know, I was delusional. I need those moments.

Him: Silent as the grave. Which reminds me... corpses?

Corpses. *Catalyst.*

So. Chronology: the idea comes in spring/summer 2015. I play with an outline that fall. I even ask for a grant from the Alberta Foundation for the Arts to write it.

But nothing's coming—actually, it's not even that it's not coming. I'm actively avoiding writing about it.

Until... November.

When I birth 15,000 words over two days.

An explosion.

I am fucking amazing.

I am not writing, by the way. I am taking dictation from God—which is a very, very rare thing for an atheist.

Oh. Yes.

Nothing has ever come to me this quickly, so easily.

Too quickly? Too easily? Don't think. Write.

Write.

Write.

Stop.

Empty.

That was... too easy.

Too quick. Too easy.

I start to distrust... the product.

And I'm right.

When I look through my output a week later, it's shit. It is all shit.

No, really, I'm not being hard on myself.

Pure melodramatic, self-aggrandizing shit. Self-indulgent to the point of making me want to vomit—no, actually, so self-indulgent that I want to slit my wrists because the person who wrote all that does not deserve to live, so self-indulgent...

Like, more self-indulgent than this project?

—If you think this project is self-indulgent, I'm not sure what you'd call *Catalyst*. That's why I'm going with *Shit*.

I throw it out.

Every single stinking word.

I actually think about printing it out so that I can stomp on it and physically shred it before throwing it out.

Instead, I just hit delete.

No!

—Yes. 15,000 words. Garbaged. Gone. SHIT.

Pause for dramatic effect.

You know that really awesome computer feature whereby the stuff you put in trash actually still exists until you empty the trash?

A priceless feature for temperamental writers.

Two weeks later, *Catalyst Draft 1* (or *Shit*, as it is now called) is still in my trash can. I retrieve it.

Maybe it wasn't so bad.

Fuck.

164

Yes, it was. Worse.

OMFG.

I have exhumed a rotting corpse.

Except…

What about…

Maybe…

Just that one section. That paragraph. If I start there, and then…

Maybe?

Maybe?

She's travelling two weekends in December, and she gives me keys to her apartment and instructions:

Write.

I obey.

The problem, I decide, is that I'm not honest enough to be able to write a memoir. A non-fiction memoir, anyway. So, what I'm going to do is write a fictionalized memoir. I'm going to call it, actually, *A Fake Memoir About the Art of Love.* Yes. And, I'm going to write it sort of in second person. As a series of letters from her (not me) to her brother (he'll be *the* metaphor). Yes. It will be brilliant.

500 words.

1,000.

4,000.

7,500…

7,522 words.

My final twenty-two words:

This isn't working. I think the problem is that there are three books here and I don't know which one I'm writing.

She comes back to her apartment, and I break her heart.

165

Her: So? How did it go? Did you write while I was away?
—7,522 words.
Her: Great!
—All but twenty-two are shit.
Her: Jane, this is getting tiresome.
—How do you think I feel?

So. I arrive in Cuba in January 2016, with two corpses inside me.

Also, all three of my children, then aged thirteen, eleven, and six.

Oh. You know I have three children, right? Have I not mentioned that I have children? Yeah. I kind of alluded to it a bit, right? I do. Three. I wasn't sure… I wasn't sure M. Jane Colette had kids. But I guess she does. Now you know.

Anyway: I'm going to solo parent for most of three months, without any kind of back up. I'm going to fully experience Cuba. I'm going to have a marvellous time.

But I'm not going to attempt to write. Maybe, a little bit of journaling. Maybe, a poem here or there. But I'm not going to stillbirth another draft of *Catalyst*. I'm not going to set myself up for failure.

I'm not going to think about *Molly Jones*.

Who…
—Shut up.

Her name is *Molly Jones*.
Fuck.
I can see her. So clearly.
Not going to think about her. Not going to write about her.

Her: I'm Molly Jones, and…

—Shut up! I'm in what's at times a Third World country, and I need to A) experience its revolution and B) hunt for food on a daily basis. Go away.

Her: I'm Molly Jones, and this is my story. Can't you see it?

I can.

I can see her. I can see how it begins. I can see it careening towards...

I'm not going to set myself up for failure.

I'm not going to write here.

Excerpt from a letter to you:

—January 17, 2016: Parenthetically, I think the book I thought I was writing in November and December has now definitely become three books—two novels and a non-fiction 'meditation,' and I'm just making notes on index cards or in my notebook as they occur to me on all three and working very hard at not trying to force any of them. Reminding myself I *just* finished a novel in August. I don't have to be halfway into another one right now...

—February 1, 2016: I think today I figured out how one of the books contained in *Catalyst* ends. Roughly. I wonder if it means tomorrow I'll start writing.

I do. I write for five weeks, every morning, for thirty to ninety minutes.

About 40,000 words, I think. All longhand. More or less in order. There are gaps, but it's a fairly cohesive first draft.

Her name is *Molly Jones*.

She's... definitely not stillborn.

QUESTION:
Do you think this is true?

IN *CONSEQUENCES*, REMEMBER, the anti-hero sets the framework for the story by telling the anti-heroine, "All tragedy is erotic. The things that make you laugh don't make you hard, or wet."

What do you think? Is that true?   .

CONFESSION 39: *I come back from Cuba and have another crisis*

LET ME JUST recap for you where I'm at.

It's April 2016.

I have a novel out that I've been ignoring pretty consistently and ardently since its publication in May 2015, and the sales of which as it approaches the first birthday of its publication are 100 per cent consistent with my level of interest in it.

I have a second novel finished—with an offer on it from Harper-fucking-Collins (except that doesn't mean what it meant to me a year ago)—and I neither want to take the offer nor begin the arduous task of finding another publisher.

And indie publishing? Forget it. Don't wanna go there. I didn't know how to promote a novel with Harper-fucking-Collins behind me.

I have a tender infant of a third novel in my suitcase. She's beautiful. I'm in love. I want to kiss her toes and spend hours tracing my finger around her ears.

I have an outrageous amount of debt because—Cuba.

I have two email messages in my inbox, asking me to contact editors/clients as soon as I'm back, because they have work for me.

I don't want to do that work, at all.

I don't want to think about *Tell Me*, at all.

I don't want to think about *Consequences*, at all.

I want to kiss Molly's cheeks. Or maybe just keep her in my suitcase.

Maybe I want to climb back into my suitcase with her. Stay there.

I don't know what to do.

I don't know who I am.

I don't want to do anything.

I should just let HarperCollins have *Consequences*. One thing off my plate, right? Then I can focus on *Molly Jones*... while they ignore *Consequences* the way they ignored *Tell Me*.

Not the smartest decision, but the easiest one, right?

I don't want to do that either.

I don't want to do anything.

THEN THIS HAPPENS:
Let us make one thing easier for you

I DON'T PARTICULARLY want to read this email from HarperCollins, either, but it's marked Urgent, so perhaps I should.

Oh. Shit.

I am writing to let you know that, as from July 1st 2016, HarperCollins has regretfully taken the decision to no longer commission new titles under the Mischief Imprint.

This decision has not been taken lightly, with both internal and external factors scrutinised.

As you know, the digital erotica market—and landscape—continues to evolve daily, but with Mischief a part of the Avon division at HarperCollins, this decision has ultimately been made as part of an overall strategic review of that division. We will therefore no longer commission front list titles, but it should go without saying that existing authors and titles on the list will be supported as usual.

…

On behalf of the team here, I'd like to thank you for your support and hard work but also for the immense contribution that you have made to Mischief and HarperCollins. I wish you well with your future writing ventures.

Kind Regards,

etc.

Well.

Shit.

How do I feel about this?

Strangely, the news is freeing.

Giving them *Consequences* is no longer an option. And *Molly Jones*, whatever *Molly Jones* is, not even A., no matter how much he might love her, could claim that she's erotica or erotic romance.

So.

I'm free, quite free.

What am I going to do?

FOR THE LAST TIME:
Reading Sylvia Plath when you're existentially angsting is a TERRIBLE idea

THESE LINES, HERE:

> *Something else*
> *Hauls me through air—*
> *Thighs, hair;*
> *Flakes from my heels.*
> *White*
> *Godiva, I unpeel—*
> *Dead hands, dead stringencies.*

Sylvia Plath, *Ariel*

make me come apart, utterly.

CONFESSION 40:
I decide to do nothing

SO I DECIDE…

I decide to do… nothing.

Except… Well, I've come back from Cuba with four volumes of notebooks and a thousand photographs. I'm going to release those—call them postcards—create a podcast around them—I need to do this ASAP, because Cuba is changing so quickly, and I need to tell this story NOW.

Also… *Molly Jones*. I need to transcribe her. Identify the holes. Fill them. Rewrite her. Tighten her. Slash her. God. Molly. You're mad. I love you. You terrify me. Is it ok to be this attached to a book, a character? What am I doing with you? Nobody, nobody can ever read you. It would be sacrilege.

What I mean, when I say I decide to do nothing is… I decide to do nothing about *Consequences*. I'm not going to query other publishers. I'm not ready to think about going indie. I didn't know how to promote *Tell Me* with the world's biggest publisher behind me—how could I possibly do it on my own?

(I've almost forgotten *Tell Me* exists. It is somewhere back there, in the past—well, really. Is that not how it should be? It is mid-2016. Three years since I finished the damn book, two years since I sold it, one year since it was published. I've moved on.)

I'm going to do nothing.

Time is on my side. The publishing world, the reading world—they are still adjusting to the e-book and Amazon revolution. Nobody really knows how to sell books. Too many writers. Too many books. I don't know what to do. Nobody knows what to do.

Whiner.
—I. Am. Not. Whining. I am taking a… pause.

And I'm writing. I'm sending the world Postcards from Cuba, and I'm tormenting *Molly Jones*. I've never done this to a book before. I take her from 40,000 words to 56,000—then slash her down to 45,000. Back to just over 50,000—and down below. And then, I add 25,000 words—they are the final, the essential ones, the ones that connect everything together—and I add them to that 50,000, and then I go through it, ruthless now, Molly, this might hurt, but now, you need to be tight, and I end up with 65,000 words.

—Is that even a novel?
Her: Well, how long were Tell Me *and* Consequences*?*

Tell Me was 103,000 words when I submitted it, and was published at 102,000—I know this, because it's in the product description at Amazon.

Consequences was 75,000… and then I took it to the mountains for a final weekend to proof it, and came back with 60,000 words.

—Did they feel like novels? I mean, when you were reading *Consequences*, did it feel long enough?

Stupid question, I know. These are the things that, a year-plus after the publication of my first novel, I still don't know: how long is a novel supposed to be, exactly? What is a novella? What should my target word count, if any, be?

Her: *Yes.* Consequences *read like a novel.* Molly Jones*, I can't tell you, because you haven't let me read it.*

Nobody's ever going to read *Molly Jones*.
It's enough that I've written her.

CONFESSION 41:
Doing nothing sucks ass

REALLY.

CONFESSION 42:
Doing nothing sucks ass 2

NOTHING, NOTHING, DOING nothing.
Doing nothing really sucks ass.
It's actually not so bad until *Molly Jones* is finished.
And then I assess my situation as such:
A. I have a published novel out there that's just kind of sitting there and not selling or doing anything.
B. I have two finished novels that are just sitting there without even having a chance of being, like… read.
C. I am doing nothing.
D. I am unhappy.
E. I am making everyone around me unhappy.

Jesus, finally. I was wondering how long it would take you to get your head out of your ass.
—Fuck off. I'm angsting here.
Get over it and figure out how you're going to sell your books.

Right.
Get over it and figure out how you're going to sell your books.
Right.

SOS:
When all else fails, consult Cheryl Strayed

THERE'S A LONG history, of women especially, saying, 'Well, I just got lucky.' I didn't just get lucky. I worked my fucking ass off. And then I got lucky. And if I hadn't worked my ass off, I wouldn't have gotten lucky. You have to do the work. You always have to do the work.

Cheryl Strayed

I have homework for you again. It's a 103-minute commitment. Find the time, and do it: look up the Cheryl Strayed interview on the Long Form Podcast, and listen to every word.

If you need to be sold on the exercise, read Maria Popova's curation of "the most shimmering parts" of the podcast on BrainPickings.org, which will make you find the time to listen to the podcast.

Then, supplement with Strayed's "Write Like a Mother-fucker" essay, which you can still find freely available on *The Rumpus* online, and then, quickly order your copy of *Tiny Beautiful Things: Advice on Life and Love by Dear Sugar*—the collection of Strayed's "Dear Sugar" columns.

(Better than *Wild*. Really.)

I don't remember—did I tell you that I saw Cheryl Strayed interview Gloria Steinem in November 2015?

Holy fuck.

Women telling stories, sharing stories.

There is nothing more powerful.

Incidentally, I'm pretty sure Gloria—and Cheryl—would both understand my a-cunt-is-not-a-pussy obsession.

CONFESSION 43:
I don't have a fucking clue how to do that

WHERE WERE WE?
Right. Here:

Get over it and figure out how you're going to sell your books.

Right.
Ok. So here's the thing. A wee problem, if you will.
I don't have a fucking clue how to do that.

Other people are doing it. All the time. Some of them well. Ask them.
—I don't know where to find them.
There's this thing called Google…
—Fuck. Off.

So yes. There is this thing called Google. And it's marvellous. When I want to know the name of the capital of Iran—Persia, as it was—during the Safavid Dynasty, or when I am teaching myself Wordpress or Scrivener, Google is my best friend. Type in the question:

How do I embed a video in Wordpress?

And someone's already asked it, and, see, there is (probably) ONLY ONE RIGHT ANSWER, and you find it, and you do it, and presto.

Type in "How do I market and promote books" into Google and you get…

Go. Just do it.

See?

Ugh.

I don't know where to start.

Him: Hold on. Aren't you, like, a professional writer? Didn't you say something about how you've been earning a living writing since you were seventeen?

Yeah.

So.

About that.

Writing for newspapers and magazines, and for corporate clients (who pay significantly more—and, in the freelance world, more promptly—than newspapers and magazines), is in many ways great training ground for any writer. I can write anytime, any place, to any unreasonable deadline—on virtually any topic.

But the business model is different. As a magazine writer and as a corporate whore—I mean, as a corporate writer—you exit as soon as you give the story to the editor or client. They pay you—and all the concerns of how to get it to the readers, and how to make money from that process, are up to them.

Additionally, my career has unfolded like this:

—I want to write.

Client 1: Here. Give me 500 words on… and I'll give you $500.

—Ok. Cool. Um… do you have any, like, 5,000-word things I could write?

Client: Sure. Do you know anything about airlines and bankruptcy law?

—No… but how hard can that be to figure out?

Not that hard, really. All stories—even business and legal stories—are, ultimately, about people.

But I digress.

Point: I don't know how to chase money. And I haven't a clue about how to sell books.

Him: How hard can that be to figure out?
—What?
Him: Just thinking out loud.

I haven't a fucking clue. I don't know where to get started. Google is an ocean of crap.

And I don't want anyone to read *Molly Jones* anyway.

Her: Jesus, Jane, get over yourself. Go find some local writers and ask them.
—Oh. Yeah. I guess I could do that.
Her: You should do that.

Right. I'll do that.
Um. How do I do that?

SOS 2: Steve Jobs gives me some advice on being naked... and dead

IT'S ABOUT THIS time that I have this intense moment with Steve Jobs. Who's already dead, which makes this insight all the more poignant:

> *Remembering that I'll be dead soon is the most important tool I've ever encountered to help me make the big choices in life. Because almost everything—all external expectations, all pride, all fear of embarrassment or failure—those things just fall away in the face of death, leaving only what is truly important. Remembering that you are going to die is the best way I know to avoid the trap of thinking you have something to lose. You are already naked.*

Steve Jobs

(quoted in *Share Your Work!* by Austin Kleon)
(which is worth reading. And not just for Jobs' quote)
(the problem with starting to write sentences in parentheses is that for some reason, it is very difficult to stop)
(it's because you've given yourself permission to create disjointed, fragmented thoughts)
(hmmm)
(so if I join two thoughts together properly and logically, the cycle will end?)
Look at that.
Now, where were we?

184

CONFESSION 44:
I hate writers

IT'S NOT THAT I hate other writers.
  I love…
  …well..
  Ok, I love *reading* other writers.
  (Also, occasionally sexting with a really good one.
Mmmm. Yes.)
  And I love artists. Fuck, I *love* artists.
  Photographers.
  The occasional poet.
  Once, a musician—but that was not good.
  I digress.
  Writers.
  I hate writers.
  Manipulative, whiny bastards who…

*Him: Don't forget narcissistic, self-indulgent, navel-gazing
assholes…*
  —Don't worry—that was coming.

I'm only partly talking about myself. I know that I'm
occasionally difficult.

  —Don't say a word.
  Him: Zipped.

185

But what I really hate about writers—is that what makes a writer is the writing.

Wait, that came out wrong. Scratch the first part. What makes a writer is the writing. Right?

A writer writes.

No other definition, expansion necessary.

Says the woman who didn't think she was a real writer until she published a novel.

—Yes, well... I have issues and need extensive therapy. We've established that.

A writer does not... whine about how he has no time to write.

Cause you've never done that?

A writer does not... whine about how there's just no point in writing because it's so difficult to get published.

Um... no, you and I have never that that conversation.

A writer does not...

I can't wait to hear this next one, you big fat hypocrite.

No! Don't call me a hypocrite: see, that's the point—who needs all that, in peers, when it's the only thing that's ever screaming in your own head?

Also, my experiences with writers tend to go one of two ways.

Version one:

I'm sitting next to her at this thing or another, one of those social encounters, planned or accidental, to be enjoyed or to be endured, we do not know yet, and we are trying to find a connection, and it usually starts with her telling me what she does, and I say...

—Cool.

and sometime that's true, and sometimes, it's a lie, and then it's my turn, and I tell her I'm a writer, and she says...

Her: What do you write?

...and this is not a question that should be difficult to answer, but it is. But I eventually manage to answer it, and, if I am feeling very brave, I end with,

—Oh. And I've also just had my first novel published.

And, oh, I fucking totally preen, wouldn't you? You would. You understand? That it's everything? The only thing that matters?
And then, she says...

Her: I'm a writer too! Oh! I MUST talk to you about that! How did you find a publisher? I don't know anything about that process! Tell me!

And I start to tell her, but then she says,

Her: I just love to write but I can't ever find the time...

...at which point I make sympathizing noises and pretend to understand, because I'm a two-faced, socially-adept liar, and steer the conversation to other topics.
But what I'm really thinking is... If you don't have the time to write... then you just don't want it bad enough. That's it, really.

It doesn't matter what it is: writing. Reading. Exercising. Fucking. Loving.

When people say they don't have the time for something, what they really mean is... they don't really want it that much.

Me... this—writing, putting stories into shape for others to read, hear, see, *experience*—is the only thing I've ever wanted.

You? What do you want, with that intensity?

That's another story.
—True. Are you going to write it?

Version two goes like this:

He's maybe got an MFA, maybe a handful of poems published in the literary magazines that carry cachet but pay no cash, but maybe not, possibly no publication credits at all, and he belongs to this organization and that, and he knows so-and-so, and such-and-such, and he's reading *The Paris Review Interviews*, and yes, Hemingway, but have I ever really tried to comprehend Gertrude Stein?

(I have. She is incomprehensible. And I'm not stupid.)

(Although I really love this exchange between Stein and Hemingway:

"It's good," [Stein] said [to Hemingway]. "That's not the question at all. But it is inaccrochable. That means it is like a picture that a painter paints and then he cannot hang it when he has a show and nobody will buy it because they cannot hang it either."

'Inaccrochable' is now one of my fave words. You see why?)

Anyway, he's a writer. He tells me all about himself. And I hope, secretly, 'Soul mate!' and I tell him about me, and about *Tell Me*, and...

—…and since then, I've finished two more novels, and now I'm trying to figure out what to do with them…

Him: Oh, are they both genre too?

—What do you mean?

Him: I mean are they both romance, erotica, whatever the genre that your first novel was in is called?

—As opposed to?

Him: Like, real literature?

Asshole.

He didn't really say that.

—No, what he actually said was, 'real books.'

And what did you say?

—"I've written three books in the last three years. What the fuck have you done?"

But not out loud.

I really should. Maybe I will next time.

Except after conversations like that happen—I never, ever want to talk to another 'writer' as long as I live.

Whiner, whiner, whiner.

—Fuck. Off.

Also, work on your people skills.

—Seriously, fuck off.

Writers.

Fucking whiners, annoying assholes, soul mates.

But. Yes. I know… I need them. I don't know what to do. I need to learn, and reinventing the wheel is stupid.

I need to find writers who… are writing. At least that. Preferably: who are writing *and* selling their writing.

K.

Let's do that.

INTERLUDE:
Why we like having sex with artists

BEING IMMORTALIZED IN *an artwork is the ultimate love letter.*
...
There's just something sexy and fascinating about someone whose daily routine deals with the sublime, and who aims to create something out of this world. It's like wanting to fuck God, kinda.
...
One minute the artist appears so amazing and confident that you can't help but open your legs, and the next minute they suddenly plummet and become vulnerable and insecure, and need you to open your arms to comfort them.

Karley Sciortino

Homework: Flirt with an artist. You don't need to end in bed with him, her, them. Just, you know, taste God. In their work, in their eyes.

ANOTHER INTERRUPTION:
What do you mean you want instructions?

JANE? I DON'T mean to complain—actually, you know what? I totally mean to complain. I thought this would be more of an instruction manual.

—What? *Like the Joy of Sex or The Whole Lesbian Sex Book or The Kama Sutra?*

No, like... you know. How to write and sell a dirty—I mean, erotic—novel. Or just how to write and sell. Something.

—Why? I told you it was no such thing, right at the outset. And if it is, the instructions are incidental-accidental—just embedded in the story, you know?

And I did that on purpose. Because, frankly, the world does not need another 'how to write' book.

I mean, seriously. The shelves sag, and the cyber-shelves are so cluttered, you can't swing a dead cat without...

Never mind. Bad, overused metaphor (which I really like, because I hate cats. Now you know).

Ok. Instructions. You want instructions.

This is what I would tattoo on my chest—if only it would be a little larger—and the chest of every other 'I want to be a writer!' person I encounter (if it weren't kind of wrong to tattoo other people against their will):

I can strive to create empowering beliefs, work on my self-esteem, and practice positive self-talk to focus my mind and affirm my power to visualize desired outcomes so as to acquire the confidence to generate the courage to find the determination to make the commitment to feel sufficiently motivated to get down to work.

Or I can just do it.

Dan Millman, *The Creative Compass*

There's unfortunately no substitute for just doing it.

But. If you need a little help in just doing it, work through Julia Cameron's *The Artist's Way*, a 12-week creative recovery course. I've mentioned her to you before, and she really helped me—the Morning Pages are magic. Really.

If there is too much God and spirituality in Julia for you: Natalie Goldberg's *Writing Down the Bones*. Goldberg wrote what may have been the first, and perhaps should have been the final, *useful* book about how to write. Everyone else is recycling.

If you have ADD (I think it's a gift and a beautiful thing; don't get defensive, look, shiny things!) and really like pretty colours: SARK's *Juicy Pens, Thirsty Paper*.

Oh, that's a good start… what else should I read?

—DON'T! That's more than enough. Stop reading and write something.

(That's me channeling Julia Cameron, who destroyed my life for a horrible week in the fall of 2014 with a reading deprivation exercise. Oh, yes. Try this: DO NOT READ FOR A WEEK. Nothing. No books. No magazines. No Facebook status updates. No news. No email. NOTHING.)

(Oh-my-fucking-god-what-am-I-doing-to-do-if-I-don't-read?
—Me and Julia: Write. You just might write.)

Wait.
Don't write.
I don't want you to write.

I want you to read. Especially my books.

Maybe I should delete this chapter...

And advice on selling? Publishing? Promoting?

—So the whole point of this story is that I don't know how to do it. And am kind of resistant to learning.

But...

—If you sit still for a few more minutes and read a few more pages, you might find your way towards a very useful appendix.

Promise?

—No. Can you stop talking now and help me focus? I'm about to go join some writers' groups and that's stressing me out, and you're adding to my stress with your demands.

I hate writers.

—Me too.

CONFESSION 45:
You know what I just realized?
This is also my coming out monologue

I HAVE... VERY bad luck finding a writerly peer group.
    I'm looking for people who:
- are writing (no matter how little time they have)
- are publishing (no matter how hard it is)
- are successful (however they themselves define that, because I haven't quite figured out what that means)

I'm looking for people... more with it than me. You know? Like me—but, um, saner. And less angsty. More practical. Over the whiny stage and onto the doing stage.

Also, I realize after my first utterly unsuccessful writers' group meeting—*nice*. Nicer than me—which, truly, shouldn't be that hard to achieve.

Also, I realize after my second ok-but-meh writers' group meeting—committed to... committed to what? Not art, not literature—I'm not looking for fanatics or idealists.

But I am looking for... fuck, you know what I'm looking for?

I've figured it out.

Workers.

Like, people who know how to grit their fucking teeth and get the job done—how to get the book finished, and then how to sell the damn book as well. I need them to

194

teach me how to grit my fucking teeth, stop whining, and learn the business side of my chosen career.

Wait.

Did you hear what I just said?

Chosen career.

Right.

Grit teeth.

Stop whining.

Her: Also, stop hating writers.

—Well. We are difficult.

You: Yup.

Her: You are adorable.

—Well. We have our moments. Also, I like *her* better than you. In case you didn't pick up on that... You did? Good.

I'm screwing, not-so-slightly, with the chronology of the narrative again, because it seems more effective to present it this way—this, by the way, is why I think many writers write—we're ultimately control freaks who like to control our reality, and whether we're building fictional worlds or crafting the way we present a non-fiction narrative, we get to exercise that control. Well, when I say 'we' ... I don't know about you, them. Me—control freak at heart. You may have noticed.

Your label for yourself. I wasn't going to say anything.

—Thank you. I've said before, white lies and carefully considered omissions are what makes the world go round.

Anyway. I actually start searching in earnest for a writers' group about the time I wake up—fall in love by the river—start writing again—in June 2014.

There is a series of... mismatches. And a couple of encounters with outright sociopaths.

Her: And you decide you hate writers. Except for me.
—I will never hate you.

And I give up.

I decide I'm supposed to be a lone wolf, and figure all this out ALL BY MYSELF.

This, I now think, is another act of self-sabotage.

And then, after about a year of no longer looking for other writers, I hear about this Queer Writers' Group.

It takes me about two, three months, to finally go.

And suddenly, I don't hate writers at all.

Her: Full of hot girls?
—A couple.

More to the point: full of people writing. Not necessarily publishing or chasing writing as career or vocation. But, writing. And wanting to write, and wanting to talk about the craft of writing, and wanting to get better.

And wanting to hang out.

Also—really, nicer than me. Nice *to* me.

I am in a safe place. It's a good place to be.

It's not, however, where I need to be—I realize that, after I come back from Cuba. It's a *safe* place. A *supportive* place. I've got a uterus/womb metaphor spinning in my head: do you see it? But that is not where I need to be.

I need to risk shit.

I need to do all those difficult things I don't want to do, don't know how to do.

Step out of my comfort zone a little further.

—That push you offered once? I think I need it.
Him: No. You've got to jump yourself.

I do.

And—I do.

CONFESSION 46:
So then I go to this conference...

THE CONFERENCE IS called When Words Collide, and it's a reader-and-writer con started by Calgary's speculative fiction writers, and designed from the beginning to include all the genres—sci-fi, fantasy, mystery, romance—as well as literary fiction, children's books, and poetry.

I don't want to go, by the way.

It's been around for five or six years in yyc. I've heard about it, of course—in those writing groups I didn't manage to join, among other places.

I've never gone or wanted to go.

Her: Because you hate writers.
—Hey, I'm trying to get over it.

I could have gone anytime over the past five years. But I've never wanted to, because—I think it's complicated, as all things are, but really it boils down to subtle and not-so-subtle acts of self-sabotage.

Voices in my head like:

—But I don't like crowds.
—I'm not very good with strangers.
—I've better things to do with my time. Imagine how much I could write over three days. And that's the really important thing.

Also…

… well, I don't want to tell you. But this is a confession.

—Genre writers? Speculative fiction writers? What could I learn from them?

—Self-published indie authors? Really? Who's giving these panels? I've never heard of any of them. What can they possibly teach me?

As the conference draws closer and closer—and I want to go less and less—I suddenly have one of these utterly unpleasant moments of clarity when I realize…

Her: You're arrogant?

Um…

Actually, it looks like arrogance—because arrogance is a very easy-to-put-on armour—but I'm actually utterly, completely insecure.

I'm terrified.

Writing is… I don't want to say *easy*, because sometimes it's not. But, in August 2016, three years after writing my first novel (and then two more in two years), I can confidently say—writing is the easy part.

Writing is completely within my control.

This other part—putting the writing into the world? Turning it into a revenue stream? Turning my vocation into a career?

I'm terrified.

I don't know how to do it.

I'm afraid I will fail at it.

Utterly.

And I'm scared.

Also, I'm not so good with strangers, and I find rooms full of people exhausting, and maybe I should take those three days and spend them writing another novel, because... that's easier.

Fuck.

I don't want to go.

I don't have to go, right?

I can just do nothing, for a while longer?

Him: Rethinking the need for that shove?

—No. I'm going. I'm jumping. Just give me a moment to catch my breath.

I go.

OMFG.

How come I haven't come to this conference before?

BY THE WAY:
Gloria Steinem told me...

WOMEN GET MORE radical with age.

Gloria Steinem
age 80, and still kicking ass

(Also, still very blonde.)
(But that's neither here or there. Is it?)

CONFESSION 47:
Maybe there was something in the water

MIND BLOWN.

I mean...

What happens is...

You know what?

I'm not going to give you a play-by-play.

I'm not even going to tell you that if you're a Calgary or Alberta writer, you should mark the second weekend of August down in your calendar, and come to next year's When Words Collide. And the one after that.

Because I don't know that it would do to you what it did for me.

You need to be open and ready for the magic to work, right?

There is magic everywhere that weekend—I am open—and it's working.

I am surrounded by people who
- are writing (no matter how little time they have)
- are publishing (no matter how hard it is)
- are successful (however they themselves define that for themselves)

I'm surrounded by people who are... 'more with it' than I am. They're over the whiny stage and onto the doing stage.

They're doing shit.

They're writing. They're publishing. They're promoting. Some well. Some badly.

(I'm judgemental, even in the middle of magic.)

It doesn't matter.

They're DOING things.

Moving.

Most importantly, perhaps: they are sharing everything they know freely and openly.

(They're so much nicer than me, see?)

I am so…

I don't know how to explain to you…

After three days of the conference, I feel so excited and so energized and so grateful, I don't fit inside my head or my body.

I'm, still, terrified.

Maybe even more so.

But I'm… I'm the opposite of paralyzed.

I. Am. Moving.

When Words Collide: whenwordscollide.org
You're welcome.

CONFESSION 48:
In conclusion, cunt is a beautiful word

IN THE TWO weeks immediately after the conference, I do more to develop my career as a fiction writer than in the preceding three years. I'll save you the play-by-play of that too (but if you want it, email me at *TellMe@mjanecolette.com* and I'll be happy to walk you through it).

Probably the most important thing that happens is that I decide to **own my genre.**

I write erotica and erotic romance. Sexy books, filthy-flirty stories. Novels that, when they do their job, leave my female readers dripping wet and my male readers hard. And I like that—that's what I want to do. With plot and story and 'social realist' lives between all the fucking… but you know what? I like writing about sex.

It's fun.

I'm good at it.

That's what Jane Austen would be doing if she was writing in 2016, and that's what Colette was doing within the looser constraints of Paris in the 1920s.

Ha.

So there.

I join the Romance Writers of America (holy fuck; the online content of the RWA University blows my mind) and its Calgary chapter, the Calgary Romance Writers Association, as well as the Alberta Romance ('We Embrace

All Genres But It's Too Complicated To Change Our Name') Writers Association.

I also join the board of When Words Collide. Because—I really can't express my gratitude sufficiently, and I want to help make that magic happen for other writers.

And, um, I start two more novels.

And I draft out a five-year career plan.

And I revisit *The Right-Brain Business Plan*, and pick up the business development work I effectively abandoned in May 2015.

And I make a lot of lists.

Like, so many, it's ridiculous.

And… I finally plan a launch party for *Tell Me*. Hey—did you go? Was it awesome? Did the burlesque dancer come?

And…

Actually, you know what? I'm going to end this story for you here, now, in this perhaps unsatisfactory place of unresolution and uncertainty—because that's where I am, right now. Making lists. Moving. Learning.

Doing all the things—but not yet seeing their results.

Crying with frustration because I have no idea whether anything I'm doing will *have* results.

Taking a very, very long-term view… then tantruming because I want results NOW.

Driving the people who love me mad.

You: Just a little.
Her: Well, kind of a lot.
Him: Valium?

Reassessing. Moving.

Terrified a truck will careen down the next intersection and flatten me again.

Moving with even more urgency as a result.

And what that end result will be…

…well, I don't know—I can't know, can I?

Here's the place that I'm trying, very hard, to keep myself in:

- I control the quality (and quantity) of the work.
- I control how I put it into the world—and I can learn how to do this better.

The outcome, the impact? Out of my hands, completely.

Partly in yours.

Partly in theirs.

Not in mine, at all.

What a terrifying, terrifying place to be.

But here I am.

Breathe.

Keep on moving.

Trying.

Learning.

Doing.

Growing.

Moving.

Are you coming with me? I can't do this alone.

...

—That was sort of the end. What? You look like you wanted to say something?

Her: I'm waiting for you to bring this back to cunts and pussies.

—Well, I was trying to building that last part towards a 'making the world safe for cunts' kind of conclusion, but it didn't happen.

Him: Do you remember, in university, when you were writing a 1500 word paper, and you saw you were about to hit the word limit, you'd just stop all your arguments and say, 'In conclusion, I've now proven my thesis and am going to end here and now?'

—Yeah. We were so fucking lazy. I can't believe profs let us get away with that. So... you want me to end this chapter with... what? 'In conclusion, cunt is a beautiful word'?

Her: Works for me.

—I'd fucking fail your ass if you did that in my class.

Her: But you're in control of this narrative. As you keep on reminding us every time any of us makes a suggestion you don't like.

—Fuck you. But you might be right.

Her: Try it.

—In conclusion... cunt is a beautiful word.

Ha.

Also, I'm going to put it in the title.

So there.

Also, give it the last word:

C-U-N-T.

Cunt.

mjc

an interjection for an
INVITATION

an interjection for an
INVITATION

IF YOU'VE FOUND this story—or any book you ever read, actually—of value, please consider leaving a review of it on the Amazon, Good Reads or Kobo sites. It's the second nicest thing you can to do help a neurotic writer.

The first being?
—Isn't it obvious? Buy our books.
Come, take the pitch all the way to the end.
—*Tell Me* is available in all the usual places, but it's best for me if you buy it from Amazon, and better yet if you buy it through my website.
Her: And Consequences?
—Do you think we should call it *Defensive Adultery*?
Her: How can you be so fucking indecisive?
—Titles are really important.

If you want to have a say in titling *The Book Formerly Known as Methadone, Now Probably Consequences—unless you like Defensive Adultery Better?* join the Rough Draft Confessions mailing list at mjanecolette.com/TellMe for sneak peaks at WIPs, cover discussion, and a chance to vote on the damn title. We still have time. (I think.)

Her: You're outsourcing the title decision to your readers?
—Did you miss Confession 2? I suck at titles.

All the marketing gurus say I should give you that "hook up with me here" URL again. Go here:

mjanecolette.com/TellMe

Thank you!

M. Jane Colette

PS An assortment of extras follows, including a few teasers (notably, the first chapter of... I'm really leaning towards *Defensive Adultery*, actually. Please help me decide!) and a couple of attempts by me to be Very Useful and to provide you with "Ten Surefire Ways to Achieve World Peace, Eternal Happiness, and Total Creative Fulfillment By Friday."
Enjoy.
And thank you, again.
Especially—*you.*
You know I always write... only for you.

PART 2

TEASERS

TEASER:
The Photograph

WHAT'S THAT?

—THIS?

Yeah. That.

—Nothing. A photograph.

I'm not blind, lover-mine, I know it's a photograph. Of whom?

—Everyone. Family. It's from Christmas.

Now there's a facet of you I did not know about. Nor suspected. Such sentimentality. Sweet.

—My sister-in-law had them printed. Gave it to me the last time I saw her, I guess. I slipped it into the iPad cover. It must have fallen out when you were rummaging through my bag for condoms.

Ha. That's more like the Elizabeth I know and fuck. The one in this photograph doesn't look like the Elizabeth I know either. Jeezus. What's wrong with your face?

—What? Nothing. I'm smiling. I'm just smiling.

Grimacing. Grinding teeth. Almost in physical pain. I've seen you smiling and in ecstasy and in pain, Liz, and—well, there's no pleasure in any part of you in this picture.

—It was a hard night. You know. Christmas. Family. High tensions. Stresses.

Tell me about it. About them. Who are all these people? My God, did you cook for all of them? In an apron? Tell me you wore an apron.

—Talking about my dysfunctional family is not going to put me in the mood to fuck again.

213

It doesn't have to. That's my job. Come on. I'm curious. And, isn't this what all women want? A lover who's passionately interested in the quotidian details of their excruciatingly boring, dysfunctional lives—as well as skilled with hands, and tongue, and cock?

—Fuck you.

You have. And if you tell me the story to my satisfaction, you will again.

—You really want to hear this?

Absolutely. The drama and tension is palpable; it jumps off the mildly fingerprinted surface. Just look at your face again. And the man next to you—is that your husband?

—That's Brian, yes.

He looks like he's restraining you, keeping you from running out of the frame. Terrified you will leave. The photograph or his life? I'm full of wonder.

—You're reading too much into a grip on an elbow.

Then correct me. And that? That's your daughter? What's her name?

—I prefer that you don't know her name.

Interesting. Understandable. But it will make telling the story cumbersome. Let's call her... Alexandra. She looks happy.

—She is. She was—it takes a lot to spoil a child's Christmas.

Next to her is?

—You insist on this?

I insist. Indulge me. Here, I'll reward you. You may keep one hand on my cock as you tell the story.

—Such a reward.

I'll put both of my hands between your legs. Stroke you when you please me.

—Pervert.

Name-calling does not please me. Who's next to... what did we call her? Alexandra. Who's next to Alexandra?

—That is Brian's ex-wife. Zia.

Gorgeous. Egyptian? And may I say, lover, your lack of jealousy pleases me. I reward you, a little.

—Ah, fuck.

Talk.

—She's as Egyptian or Arab as I am French. Canadian, in other words. Born here. As for lack of jealousy... well, it wasn't my idea to have her there, for Christmas. It was the first time that's happened in fifteen years. But you're pushing ahead of the story.

Indeed. I'm impatient. You know that. Still. We should do this properly. Continue with the cast of characters. Kneeling at her feet? Love that pose, of course.

—That's Stefan. He... well, that's hard to explain. In that moment, in that photograph, he'd be Zia's... boyfriend.

Such a juvenile word when used in relation to a man fucking a fifty-year-old woman. Lover?

—Well... that depends on what you understand by the word.

I can't wait for you to explain that part of the story. The wife, the husband. The daughter. The ex-wife. Her—ha!—boytoy boyfriend. This angry young woman—the only person in the picture in more pain than you, lover—this must be the daughter of the first marriage?

—Yes. That's Brian and Zia's daughter.

Her name?

They called her Destiny. But she... she changes her name, later. When Alexandra is born. To Sasha.

Destiny-Sasha. And I get to know her real name? Mmm. Fascinating. I'm allowed to know the stepdaughter's real name. Does she hurl accusations of favouritism and evil stepmotherness at you?

—All the time.

As she should. Now, this woman? She's the reason I'm forcing you to tell the story, you know. As soon as I looked at the picture, she jumped out as its centre, focus. And yet, there she is, at its edge. Almost out of frame.

—I have to stop fucking artists with high EQ. Yes. That's what she is. The centre. The focus. That's Annie. My sister-in-law. Brian's brother's wife. She's the reason—she was the glue that made us a family. And the catalyst... Fuck, I don't

215

know how to explain it. She's the reason—the reason everything unfolded as it did, I think.

Catalyst? Everything? This gets better and better. And you wonder why I want to hear the story. But wait. There's Brian's brother's wife. And where, I must ask, is Brian's brother?

—Oh... you're right, he's not there. He was there, I'm sure he was there. Right. He must be taking the picture.

Brian's forgettable brother. Does he have a name? Wait—don't tell me. Not yet. I like him nameless, behind the camera, in the shadows. So. That's the cast. Now put the picture over there, in that bowl of walnuts... and now, both hands on my cock. And tell me everything. I won't distract you too much. Except when you get to the really good parts.

—I have no idea where to begin.

At the beginning, of course. At the photograph.

—That's not the beginning. That's practically the end.

Well. Then begin with the thing that's most important to me. When you met me. It must have been around that time. I recognize the haircut. And those shoes.

—We met a few weeks later, yes. But you're not part of the story. Not at all.

You're so wrong. Every story before you met me is the backstory to... well, why you're here. In my hotel room. Naked. Beside me. Beneath me. With me. So it's, really, all about me.

—Narcissist.

I prefer sociopath. Still. I'll indulge you. Never mind me. Start with her.

—Her? Annie?

Yes. She is the catalyst, you said? Anyway. She is where you should begin. I want to know her intimately.

—I don't. I didn't.

But you do, don't you? So. Talk. But keep in mind... I'm easily bored. And I only really like one type of story.

—Am I telling a story to you or to your cock?

We are fully integrated. One and the same. And what a perfect feedback loop you have. Now. Impatient. Begin. Tell me about you and Annie.

—Then I have to tell you about me and Brian. Brian and Zia. Zia and Annie… All of them, all of us.

Hmmm. All right. Go ahead. But start the story with something hot.

—How about a thoroughly inappropriate photograph, texted to the wrong number?

I love it. Go.

*

That is how *Consequences (Defensive Adultery)* begins.

What do you think?

Teased?

Coming Spring 2017.

(Also, seriously—*Consequences*… or *Defensive Adultery*? It's killing me. Help me decide. I'm pretty sure we still have time.)

TEASER:
A Walk In The Woods

THIS PIECE IS an outtake from *Consequences/Defensive Adultery*.

You made me cut it, on your second read-through. You were right. It broke the flow, it didn't fit—it's out of character, Annie would never, ever... And taking it out also fixed that pacing error I had been struggling with.

So thank you.

But here. It's not so bad, on its own, and I thought *she* might enjoy it too.

*

And if it were possible? If we hadn't made our choices, closed other doors? What would you do?

—I would seduce you during a walk in the woods. But I would let you think you were seducing me.

Oh, I like how that starts. Spin the story.

—Stories are dangerous.

I don't care. I'm willing to sin, and sin big, in a story.

—We would meet for coffee... No, not like that. I've got a workshop downtown I'm doing, and you would text me from your office. You would say, I need to get out of here. Come play hooky with me.

I like that. Big sins start with little sins. Skipping work.

218

—You have meetings, deadlines. I have that workshop. We slough them off—I grab purse, jacket, make some sort of excuse. Meet you in the parkade.

What are you wearing? An expensive business suit that will soon be covered with green stains?

—Sure… thoroughly inappropriate for a walk in the woods. White, to boot. But you say, when you see me, "Let's go to Griffith Woods."

Love GW. When we get to the parking lot, is there a blanket in my trunk?

—No.

A gentleman would bring a blanket.

—You are no gentleman. Also, you have premeditated nothing. This is just a walk. Like that walk in the Devonian Gardens we're planning.

A walk. In the woods.

—Yes.

I think, in the back of my mind, I have an ulterior motive.

—Perhaps. And in the back of mine, I have secret hopes, fantasies.

Not so secret, anymore. So, we walk? No blanket?

—We walk. Talk about all the usual things. I walk a little ahead of you when the path narrows. I know I'm posing. Arching. Tensing.

I love it. I take out my phone—every once in a while, I take a picture. Not of the scenery.

—Every once in a while, I trip—accidentally-on-purpose—and clutch at you.

So innocent. Yet so obvious. I'm getting excited. You need to speed up the seduction.

—All I'm doing is creating the opportunity for you to seduce me. But all right. "Let's rest here."

Too close to the main path. I take your hand and lead you deeper into the woods.

—My heart pounds.

Mine too. Am I actually going to do this?

219

—You are. There's a blown over tree sheltered by Saskatoon bushes. I sit on the stump, look up at you.

I can see it... As I'm not a gentleman, the first thought in my head is to shove my cock into your mouth.

—Christ...

But instead, I stoop down, kneel on the moss beside you.

—You look at me, and all I want is for you to kiss me. The tension...

The tension... There is no air between us, just lust.

—I lean in... I want to kiss you.

I know. I evade your lips and drop between your legs.

—I hear rustling! Someone's coming!

I don't care. I haven't even started...

—Oh!

*

The reason they made me cut it... is that it's a near-500 words set-up for this bit (which I'm keeping):

The thing about fantasy—about words on the screen—is that every risk is imaginary. There is only excitement. The other hikers don't walk in on you, don't see a white flaccid ass shaking as it thrusts. They come upon the scene at the perfect moment—when she's come, and he's come, and her shirt is pulled down and his pants are done up, and maybe they're dishevelled and maybe it looks suspicious— maybe—but that's hot, and it's all ok. Everything is ok.

There is no penalty.

There is always a happy ending.

...which, as it turns out, works just fine without the set-up.

Moral of this story: beta readers RULE. And, you should always kill your darlings. (But then, maybe, repackage them.)

TEASER:
Molly Jones

ACTUALLY...
  NO.
  I'VE changed my mind.
  I'm not ready.
  You don't get even the smallest taste of her yet.
  Sorry.
  Um.
  You can have a lick of this instead...

*

Thirty-year-old Cassandra breaks up with her long-time boyfriend and business partner at her mother's funeral. Homeless and effectively unemployed, she moves into the house she inherits from her mother, only to find her mother has engaged in a bout of deathbed matchmaking and left her entire estate—both house and business—jointly to Cassandra and her ex-lover Sylvia, with executor power in the hands of a too-smart, too-good-looking, too-arrogant lawyer, whom Cassandra wants to strangle on first sight.

The romantic drama—and comedy—that follows plays with the Sylvia-Cassandra-Raj/Roger—that's the lawyer's name—triangle, and others as well. The personality of Cassandra's deceased mother casts a long shadow over the action: she's a flamboyant figure who married and divorced five times, built herself an outrageously successful career as a psychic, astrologer, and Tarot card reader, defied every existing convention—and somehow, raised an extremely conventional daughter. Inheriting her mother's New Age business and list of devoted Tarot clients is not the career Cassandra—a software programmer by training—had in mind. Having Sylvia thrust back into her life is even worse: it had been a passionate affair in their youth, but Sylvia had made it clear that motherhood and a white-picket-fence-nuclear family, however queer, were not in her life plans—and Cassandra desperately wants babies.

Raj/Roger (child of Pakistani immigrants, he's got a bit of a cultural identity crisis) doesn't. Even if he wasn't so infuriating—he rubs her the wrong way with every encounter—he's not only made it clear he doesn't want more children, but he acts as if he wishes he didn't have the one he had.

Cassandra *hates* him. And she doesn't understand why untangling her mother's estate is taking so long… or why he keeps on coming back for Tarot card readings that she's unqualified to give and he doesn't believe in—and how do the intermittent sparks with Sylvia fit into all of this?

*

That's the pitch for *It's All In The Cards*. What do you think? It's an ass-backwards exercise for me… I had a sudden opportunity to present a pitch to an editor of a major publishing house, and so I took *Cassandra*, who's been kicking around in my head for a while, and made her conform to the required outline. Killed off her brother and entire extended family in the process.

But it sort of works.

And, the editor liked it.

It is (it will be?) my first novel centred on a single (that is, not married) and childless heroine.

Oh, this one will be fun and easy to write.
Molly Jones... Molly Jones hurt.
Hurt so much, it felt like bliss in the end...

TEASER:
Text Me, Cupid

THIS IS ANOTHER idea I'm working with now—the working title is *Text Me, Cupid*—and it's early days yet, but I wanted to show you how I work with a story when I'm getting to know it.

*

I am trying to get to know a character named Florence. No, that's wrong. Florence, I know intimately, I can see her so clearly… and I can see how the story begins. Florence and Will—but I need to change his name, I know too many Wills, and the associations will wreck havoc on the one I am imagining—are in Café Blanca. She gets there first—she always gets places first. She sits in the spot that I think of as my office away from home—home away from the office. She also sits in the 'masculine spot'—did you know, by the way, that that's a thing? I didn't, until I went out for drinks with a Persian boy who made me switch spots.

"That's the guy's place," he said.

"Really?" I raised my eyebrows. "Why?"

"Back to the back to the room, eyes to the front—you see who's coming and going—it's the place of control."

"Really?" I said. Still sitting. I looked around—yes. I had the vantage point—I could see everyone and anyone who came into the bar, who approached our table.

"Is that where you usually sit?" he asked me. I had to think about it, but the answer was, of course... yes.

"See, I've only known you for five minutes, and I already know you like to be in control," he said. "We're going to change that."

^^^*I like where that is going, too. But that's not part of the story I'm massaging today. But, it will be part of another story, one day—and it is already, always part of mine.*

So. Florence. Café Blanca. She's sitting with her back against the window, with a view of the café. And she's there first. She sees him come in...

...but all of that will unfold in their conversation... The way the story will start on paper, what the reader will first see is this:

"This is not going to work out," she said.

"What?" I flinched. "What did you say?"

"This is not going to work out," she said. "Don't you think?"

It's been ten minutes. I've been sitting opposite this woman for ten minutes... and already? This?

"I thought it was going rather well," I said. Stupid. Awkward. Shouldn't have said anything. Should be silent.

"Oh, you're very sweet," she said. Smiled. Fuck. Beautiful smile—I loved her smile. "And cute," she added, leaned across the table, made incredible eye contact that made me...

"But it's not going to work out," she said. Smiling. And looking into my eyes.

What the fuck?

"Say it," she invited me.

"What?"

"You just thought something angry. Obscene?" she asked. Eyebrows up. "Did you call me a bitch? Or something worse?"

225

"I just thought... 'what the fuck,'" I said. "I thought... I thought it was going quite well. This."

"It is," she smiled. "You're sweet. But it's not going to work out. I already know."

"Why not?" I asked.

"Because," she smiled—fuck, why did she keep on smiling? I needed her to stop smiling so I could hate her. "Because," she smiled again, "you're sweet. And I'm not."

*

Florence is going to be such an awesome character. You will love her. Or hate her. Probably both.

Dialectics.

(Did you Google dialectics the last time I brought it up? No? Go do it now.)

TEASER:
What puts you in the mood to fuck?

HERE, NO PRE-amble. Let's go straight to this:

*

—May I be blunt?

Her: Of course.

—Are you sure? You haven't really seen me blunt yet.

Her: Now I'm afraid.

—Good. May I be blunt?

Her: ...

—Yes?

Her: Yes.

—What puts you in the mood to fuck?

For me, it's words. Obviously. Words in a book, words on a screen. Words in my head. Words in your mouth, oh, your tongue...

Pictures? Thoroughly unnecessary. But part of the reason I wrote *Tell Me...* was because I can't find the sorts of words I need, want, very often.

Have you found them?

If you have, I really want to know.

My experience with erotica that really works for me is pretty limited. And so, so catholic. There is, of course, Angela Anaïs Juana Antolina Rosa Edelmira Nin y Culmell.

That is, the one and only Anaïs Nin. Get a copy of *The Delta of Venus* and *Little Birds*. Don't borrow someone else's—I know where their hands have been. (I occasionally dally with Henry Miller, too, but only because he was Nin's lover.)

Also: Colette. She didn't exactly write erotica… but Christ. Could she write. She changed literature more than any other woman writer since Jane Austen. Speaking of… imagine, just imagine, how much better the incomparable Austen would have been if she had A) given birth (at least once) B) fucked rapaciously, passionately, recklessly (repeatedly).

Oh, Miss Austen.

Where was I?

—What puts you in the mood to fuck?

Right. I want to know who you read. Who excites you, pleases you. Makes you cum, with words alone.

Teach me about my creative cohort.

Her: I am your creative cohort. Have you not read my books?
—Are you? Have I not? Educate me. I want to learn.

So. Please. Tell me your story. What you like to read. Who you like to read.

Her: I'm flushed. Embarrassed.
—Beloved. Why? Talking—writing about sex the way real people experience it is one of the most radical acts a woman can engage in. It will change you; it will change the world.

This is going to be a game on my blog in 2017. With some more rules and guidelines to be revealed shortly. You should come play:

mjanecolette.com

PART 3

A VERY USEFUL APPENDIX

USEFUL THING 1:
Priorities, baby, priorities—or, 'I don't' as an answer to 'How do you do it all?'

THIS IS A post from September 9, 2015 by my Mommy Blogger self, and whether you're struggling with finding time to write or to read (or just to live)—this post will help you. Really.

It's possibly the only useful thing on writing (living) I've ever written.

Enjoy.

*

I finally figured it out, and so I'm going to tell you. You see...

Ender: Mom! Where are you?

...you've been asking me for years, "How do you do it?" And what I thought you were asking was "How do you work *and* take care of your children; how do you write *and* homeschool" and variants on the above...

Flora: Moooom! Where are you? Ender wants you!

231

…and I would tell you, and you'd get this glazed and confused and frightened look in your eyes, and never actually—so it seemed to me—hear anything I said— certainly in no way *heed* my un-advice. But I had this immense epiphany the other day…

Cinder: Mooooom! I want to make cookies; where the hell is the margarine?

…that is was *my* fault—I wasn't telling you what you needed to know, because I wasn't hearing what you were asking. You see, while I thought you were asking…

Flora: Mom, Ender just stole my orange marker, tell him he has to give it back!
Cinder: Hey, Mom, can you wash the good cookie sheet? It's covered with chicken grease.
Ender: It's! Not! Fair!

…while I thought you were asking, "How do you find the time to write and take care of the kids and take care of the house and exercise and have a life and, and, and," what you were actually asking…

Flora: Mom, Ender won't leave me alone!
Ender: Mom, Cinder pinched me!
Cinder: Mom, the little bugger stole my Lego guys again!

…what you were actually asking is…

Ender: Maaaaaa…
—Jane: Shut up, shut up, shut up! GET OUT OF HERE! Now! Outside! All of you! Give me thirty minutes, and then you can come talk to me. Now—out. OUT!
Flora: Mom, it's like zero degrees out. And raining.
—Jane: OUT!

232

Cinder: Maybe she just means out of the room.

—Jane: OOOOOOUUUUUTTTTT!

Ender: But I'm hungry!

—Jane: There are bananas and bagels in the kitchen. GET! OUT! AND STOP ASKING ME FOR SHIT! OUT! NOW!

...what you were asking me was "How do I work (write) *while* interacting meaningfully with my children *while* making amazing dinners *while* keeping a clean, no, an *immaculate* house *while* pursuing my personal interests ALL AT THE SAME TIME."

Yeah. So, the answer to that...

I DON'T.

YOU CAN'T.

YOU WON'T.

If you have this picture in your head of your laptop computer on the kitchen table, and you writing a novel—or, fuck, even a 1500-word article—*while* washing the dishes, peeling potatoes *and* teaching your children math *and* having a meaningful conversation with your lover...

Cinder: Are you done yet? About that baking tray...

—Jane: Clean it yourself or make chicken-flavoured cookies, I don't care, leave me alone!

Flora: Is she done?

Cinder: No, she's still pissy.

—Jane: Writing! I'm still writing!

Cinder: Writing, pissy. It's kind of the same thing.

—Jane: Only when you interrupt me. NOW GO AWAY!

...you are dooming yourself to failure, because all those 'whiles' are impossible.

You know this intellectually, right? You can't, oh—have a shower WHILE typing on your laptop. Make risotto WHILE scrubbing the kitchen floor. Paint a bedroom wall WHILE having sex.

So. You can't write (work) WHILE interacting meaningfully with your children (or cleaning house or making supper or buying groceries or doing yoga or…)

Now, you CAN—I do—do most of these things sequentially, at different parts of the day-week-month.

But…

You will do some better than others.

And choosing to give time to some things will mean less time for others.

Priorities, baby.

Of course, you know this, intellectually, right? But practically… you never seem to hear me. You know, like when I tell you what a crappy housekeeper I am, or that my children eat cucumbers and mustard as snacks when I'm on deadline? And you think I'm being funny?

The truth: say, I have two hours. In those two hours—I can write a story—edit a chapter—craft a rough draft of a pitch.

Or. I can make risotto.

(I don't, by the way, know how to make risotto. But I understand it involves standing at a stove for an eternity, stirring a pot of rice. *Fuck. That.*)

Or. I can scrub the kitchen floor and the stairs. Or, do laundry or make the beds or declutter.

Or, read a chapter or two of *Harry Potter* or *Hank the Cow Dog* or *Wow! Canada* to the kids, teach Ender to read, help Cinder with his math…

These are all things that I *should* do, and *do* do at some point in a week (month… year… except that risotto thing, that's just NEVER going to happen).

But if what I need to do—want to do—with those two hours is write a story… then I have to use those two hours to write the damn story.

And that may mean ensuring other-adult child care for my children.

—Jane: Moooom! I'm on deadline, can you please come and take the monsters AWAY for a while BECAUSE THEY WILL NOT LEAVE ME ALONE!

Or, leaving the house for two hours for a nearby coffee shop, so that the house—"The fridge really needs cleaning today, Jane, it does, it does, clean me!"—doesn't make its passive-aggressive demands on me.

And, picking up a roast chicken or frozen pizza from the grocery store on the way home instead of making the perfect, healthier pizza crust from scratch (this, by the way, I can do and I do do… just not on deadline days, y'know?).

I have become much better at this over the years. Accepting that my time and energy are limited—as are yours—and becoming better and better at channeling that time and energy into the things that are really important to me.

So. I write. Every day. (Really. Sometimes, utter crap. But. Every. Day.)

Read with my kids. Take them on amazing adventures. (Most days.)

Exercise religiously, no matter how urgent the deadline, because, health.

Make guilt-free time for my friends and loves and just for myself, too—but not so much for organizing the Tupperware drawer (or for people who drain me).

Scrub the kitchen floor only when it gets to THAT level of filthy—or I desperately need to procrastinate (sometimes, that happens).

Never, ever make risotto.

Cinder: You done yet?
—Jane: Two minutes.

(I think, by the way, that if making risotto is an essential part of **who you are and need to be**, you will find a way to make risotto AND write AND take care of your kids *and* all those other things. You will maybe let something else slide more than I do. Read less, stir more. Stay home more—the stirring demands it—and skin your knees in the wild less.)
Priorities, baby.

Cinder: Hurry. I didn't scrub the tray that well, the chicken fat caught fire and I can't turn off the smoke alarm.
—Jane: Coming.

Priorities.
You're welcome.

xoxo
"Jane"

USEFUL THING 2:
Meditation for writers, 'Mom! I need you!' and struggling to stay on that tightrope

THIS IS A post my Mommy Blogger self wrote in October 2014, when she had begun the Morning Page habit—and had just finished the first draft of *Methadone-Consequence-Defensive Adultery* (I'm sorry! Titles are hard!). I include it here for you, because it's the second most useful thing I've ever written—at least from the point of view of a writer-who-is-also-mother (and all those other things).

*

I walk the tightrope, a kid on each arm for balance.

Vera Pavlova
If There Is Something To Desire

For Deb, who wanted more naked. For Jen, who cannot ever stop writing. For Katia, who's about to start a new job... because life was not intense enough as it was, was it, darling? For Cathy, who feels guilty about thinking—and who *needs* to start writing. For my Nicole, whose tightrope is harder than mine. For Nan, who understands too well—and, of course, with gratitude for the introduction.

And for *you*. Because that tightrope I walk? Nothing unique about it, is there?

CAVEAT: This is a 3000+ word post and thus a ridiculous online time commitment. And it's not the type of piece you skim for the funny bits. So. Go get yourself a glass of wine. (Some University of Alberta professors have just discovered that drinking wine has the same health benefits as going to the gym—finally! Good news!) Put on some hot shoes...

(You don't need to, but it will make me happy. What? You think this should be about you, not about me? Fine. Sit there in your slouchy, holey socks. I wrote this in knee-high gladiator sandals—black, leather, strappy—just to make you happy. But whatever. You're the reader. Do what you like. Oh, sweetness. Thank you. Thank you. I love them!)

...get the children watching *James and The Giant Peach* on Netflix. And let's get naked.

...

I.

Today, I am writing sitting criss-cross apple sauce on the couch, wearing a jacket that smells of camp fire smoke, two hairy blankets wrapped around my bare, chilled (and also hairy) legs. Next to me is the almost five-year-old, with soy chocolate milk stains on his pants and joy in his heart, because he just ate four mandarin oranges for breakfast.

He's watching *Blue's Clues*.

I'm meditating.

(Yes. I lied about the hot shoes I was wearing when writing this post just to get you to put yours on. I'd apologize... but here you are, all dressed up. And don't you feel good?)

Which means, I am writing the longhand version of this post—perverting the instructions of Julia Cameron's *The Artist's Way*, subverting the wisdom of Naomi Goldberg's *Writing Down the Bones*, and making Sarah Selecky's daily writing prompts entirely my own...

You're confused. It's all right. I'm confused and confusing. Walk with me a little, and let's confuse each other some more.

For the last two, near-three months, I've been starting my days with Sarah Selecky. Selecky is a Canadian writer, author of *This Cake is for the Party*, and creator of The Story is A State of Mind and The Story Intensive courses, which she promotes, *inter alia*, through a free daily writing prompt. I was introduced to her work the first time I met a new crush. Have you ever witnessed two writers getting to know each other? Only two questions seem to really matter: *who* are you reading? And... what are you writing?

But I wasn't writing anything—not anything that *mattered*. I was... stalled? Stalled. Paused. It was at the tail-end of that awful-no-good post-flood Lost Year. I was so tired... and also, so tired of not moving. Of the brilliant (or was it? No, it just sucked, that's why it wasn't going anywhere...) idea I had for my second novel—oh-yes, what a perfect way to further subvert convention-expectation-story—remaining a chaotic, one-page mind map and a 1500-word teaser that was NOT. GOING. ANYWHERE. It was never going to go anywhere, because I was too-stupid-lazy-talentless to do anything with it, the idea was too ambitious—no, it was too trite, too cliché, so not worth writing about—too hard to write about... except I could not write about anything else because all that swirled in my head was this...

"Sarah Selecky's writing prompts," she said, for perhaps the sixth (or sixtieth?) time that we had that same conversation.

"What?"

"Sarah. Selecky."

She didn't say, "Try it." Or—what anyone else would have said, what *I* would have said had the situation been reversed, "Stop your whining and try this..."

I finally heard her *that* day because I had just met the yyc artist Amy Dryer, and I fell in love with her work, her process, her courage—and oh, her studio, her studio! ...

Because of my encounter with Dryer, I was, very briefly, open to thinking about myself as an artist who needs to create. It's a state I resist, because... well, pretentious, right? I am so not an artist. Part of my amateur-professional dichotomy—and I've internalized that too well—is also artist-professional. And I am a *professional*—the definition of professional being showing up and doing the work even when you don't want to, and doing it so well, even when you don't care, don't want to, that no one can tell the difference.

I don't wait for inspiration.
I PERFORM on demand.

Except, I wasn't. Instead: flailing. Wailing. *Not* doing the work I really wanted to be doing. And sick of being a wanker.

So.

Amy. Artist, for sure. Me? Maybe? Sometimes? Open, opening. Inspired. And the rivers crested but stayed in their banks, and I had, while not a room of my own, once again a space-that-is-me-my-heart-mind-made-into-place, and it was time to unpause. To move. To write the thing I needed to write.

But. Inertia. Stalled. Help.

Phone. Where is my phone?

Text: "What is the name of that writer you keep on telling me about? The one who has those creative writing prompts?"

She texts back: "Sarah Selecky, at sarahselecky.com."

I love her, because she doesn't say—about time.

I do the thing. Sign up for the writing prompts. Tell myself—tomorrow morning, when I wake up, I will write.

Morning: I check my email. And there it is.

"Write about mica. Write by hand, in your notebook, for ten minutes."

And... panic. By hand? On paper? With—really—*ink*?

I used to write by hand a lot. Journals. Sketches. Vignettes. Documentation of my children's earliest years. Outlines of my first, terrible-no-good novels. First drafts of short stories. And letters. Letters to you—did you keep them? Everything you ever wrote to me is gone. ...

...and, really? By hand? In 2014?

I don't even have a notebook.

What an excuse, what a perfect excuse, not to start.

No excuses.

I find one of my kids' unfinished composition books. Find a blank page. A pencil.

Mica.

No.

I don't want to write about mica. What's mica, even?

I want to write my novel.

I want to write about cold Elizabeth, connecting Annie, crazy Zia, and angsting Destiny—why did Zia give her daughter such a terrible name? Right, there was a reason... I had a reason for that... Oh. Right...

Write.

I put Elizabeth and Annie on a rocky Alberta beach where the water shimmers with mica. And Annie bursts in tears, and Elizabeth is appalled, and I write two awkward, stilted, AWFUL pages.

Done.

(and at this moment, during that day's writing meditation, Ender is done too, and demands I read him Ten Apples Up On Top, *and I do, and I write no more, about anything, that day. The next day, I pick up, here...)*

II.

The next day, I "describe the smell of coconut sun tan lotion without using the word sweet" in three terrible

(AWFUL, UNUSABLE) pages that show how much Elizabeth resents Annie's attempts to have a relationship with her daughter. The day after, four scenes about walnuts—Elizabeth and Brian's biggest fight, Annie's most generous gift, a hint at Elizabeth's secret life…

The writing gets easier. And my days get easier. Even on the ones when life's demands prevent me from sitting down at the computer ever—or limit my writing sessions to urgent professional transactions (prose for cash, propaganda for cheques, what story do you need me to sell to your clients today, client of mine?), I feel like I have written. And to purpose, *my* bigger purpose.

I have written, I have been a writer—now I can be all the other things. Perform on demand…

I know I've established a sustainable habit when, on a day we all have to get up at 5 a.m. in order to get three kids and two adults into a car by 6 a.m. for an eight-hour car trip—the first thing I do when I wake up is take ten minutes to sit and write.

Two months later, I have, in two and a half notebooks, and on a few assorted scraps of paper torn out of other people's notebooks ("Seriously, Mom?" "I'm sorry! I couldn't find my notebook." "Again?") a rough—chaotic, messy, non-linear, and oh-with-so-many holes—draft of a novel. It needs so much more work…

But it's just pulsating with potential.

I am pulsating with gratitude. For Sarah and her prompts. Amy the artist and the permission she gave me, for a few hours at least, to think of myself as such. The writer-who-introduced-us, for her persistence and gentleness of suggestion.

I pervert-subvert-harness Selecky's process. I turn the prompts into kickstarts to get me writing about something I already know I want-to-need-to write about. When she tells me to make lists, I write dialogues between Elizabeth and Annie. When the writing prompt is to "Write about a

242

character named Wire," I create a lover for Sasha (that's Destiny's new name; she aggressively rechristened herself when the prompt was "Write a scene set under a hanging pendant lamp," and what a surprise that was). He's awful. He appals her mother. Amuses her stepmother. Sasha dumps him the day Elizabeth tells her she thinks he's "quite attractive. Reminds me of your father."

Elizabeth is a bitch. Actually, more. Another word is much more appropriate... (My publisher raises his eyebrows. "Again? We have to talk about *that* word again?" Maybe. We'll see...)

I love her.

When Selecky tells me to describe my mother from the point of view of my father, I, for once, do what I'm told. I follow instructions, precisely. How can I resist?

By mid-September, I don't need the writing prompts. Most days, I sit down and just write. Sometimes, bits for the book. Occasionally, like now, skeletons or blueprints for posts or essays. More often, I just sketch with words. Sometimes, it flows. Sometimes, it hurts. Sometimes, I dive into my email for the writing prompt, because I am stuck, don't know quite how to begin that day. Other times, I ask my kids to throw random words at me to get me started.

It's not easy.

I don't mean the writing. Writing is sometimes easy and sometimes not, like everything in life. I mean—it's not easy DOING it. Finding, having, maintaining the space-and-time to do it.

That's the tightrope I walk... Do you walk it too?

III.

A month—less—into my new writing routine, Sean has a mini-breakdown about it. Me, at the kitchen table, with my notebook. Writing. Every morning, no matter what else is happening. What does that mean?

I don't understand.

He unravels. What is he supposed to do during this time? With himself? With the kids? Is he not supposed to start work until I finish? Is he...

Interrupted in my flow, I am rage and anger and so-not-Zen.

"I don't give a fuck what you do. Just let me write. Don't talk to me until I finish."

"But... the children..."

The children are twelve, nine, and almost five.

"They can tend to themselves while I write for ten, fifteen—hell, thirty minutes. Why are we even talking about this? It is not a big deal. Nobody is affected!"

Except... they are.

I have been typing-writing, in spurts, bits, wrested minutes of time, negotiated, blocked-off hours of time, computer in lap, on table, all of my children's lives—the entire duration of my marriage.

My writing has been, *is,* my work; it helps pay for our house, our food, our life.

My pre-write-by-hand-in-your-notebook-for-ten-minutes morning routine involved having my computer in my lap. Facebook, email, blogging maintenance-and-business. Reading online news.

Why is this—me, notebook, kitchen table—different? Why is it a big deal?

Sean can't tell me, in that moment. But we figure it out, as we talk about it, and when I realize—that I'm not just writing. **That this time in the morning, bent over my notebook—this is my meditation. Prayer. And it really works.** It is perfectly effective for me—even when it's hard, slogging.

What that means: **I am completely in the work. I am fully present** *there.* **And so—fully absent elsewhere.**

I don't notice Sean when he comes into the kitchen and asks me if I want a cup of coffee.

I don't say hi to Flora when she wanders in to get her bowl of cereal. I don't even see her.

Ender climbs onto my shoulders, seeking attention and affection... and I shrug him off and keep on writing.

And I do all this not in the space-that-is-me-my-heart-mind-made-into-place—the place where I'm *supposed* to write... but in the kitchen. The place where they think I should be *theirs*.

Flora captures their perception of what's happening too aptly one day on a beach on the Haida Gwaii. The psychic who lives next door and who is our *cicerone* on that trip to the edge of the world and beyond comments what a wonderful, involved, loving, and physically engaged mother I am. (She's like that, my psychic-neighbour-beloved-friend-of-many-lifetimes, so good at handing out compliments, just when they're needed—were only more of us like her.)

"Very unusual for a Gemini," she adds. "They tend to be more detached. More in their heads."

I flush with pleasure. And my Flora wraps her arms around me from the back, and kisses my cheek.

Mommy loves us so much and she loves hugging and being hugged and kissing and playing,

she says, squeezing me hard. She pauses.

Except when she's writing. Then she wishes we'd all go away and die.

She laughs.
I burst into tears.
Because it's true.
Not the 'and die' part. Gods, not that, never. But this 'go away and leave me alone I'm writing!' part?
Yes.

245

IV.

My friend L.A. is working on a paper about post-modern feminist discourse on domestic violence and from within this research, throws this quote into my newsfeed:

It is important to place ambivalence at the heart of mothers' relationships with their children. In this analysis, mothers both love and hate their children and this ambivalence can contribute to creative, thoughtful mothering.

I ponder. I don't think I am ambivalent about my children. I love them ferociously, desperately. Life without them is untenable; I no longer have any conception of myself without this exhilarating-exhausting-never-ending— childhood may be a stage; motherhood is forever—role. I would do it all again, more or less the same way (I would have had Ender sooner) a hundred, a thousand times.

But there is no doubt that what they want and need is often in conflict with what I want and need.

The more so as I get older.

'Mother' is NOT my all-encompassing identity.

Neither is 'wife.'

(And housekeeper-housewife-homemaker don't even come into play…)

And I will be neither a martyr nor a negligent parent. So…

I am struggling—do you see that? Because I don't want to pretend, through pretty words, that I have the answers to anything here—I am struggling, as never before, to fulfill-discharge my obligations to my children and my family *and* my obligations to myself. And maybe you are too. You know how they tell you it gets easier? They lie. In so many ways, it gets harder.

(What? No, no, don't take off your shoes. You're almost at the end. And you look sooo good. Come on, love. If you're going to do this, do it properly. It's not like you're dancing or standing in them, right? Just lounging on the couch. Put your perfectly shod feet up—there, you

can admire them and yourself better in that position—and… let's continue…)

There was a time, not that long ago, when my meditation was baby-at-breast… or walking a stroller around the block, and writing in my head, and that was… not perfect, but enough. Because, the smell of the baby's head, the curl of those tiny fingers around my thumb fed me as nothing else.

And also… because what the baby needed from me… was so very simple. So very physical…

When they need me now, they don't need just the breast, the arms, my body. For Ender, that's still key, but it's shifting even there, and for the older two—they either don't need me at all (but, inevitably, that is when Ender needs me most) or they need me so fully-completely, letting my mind wander-and-write-as-it-wants-to isn't an option.

And I need me, in the moments I write, fully-completely too. The work and writing I want to do now is more difficult (rewarding), challenging (ambitious). It requires more of me. I want to give more to it.

So. There we are. Ambivalent? No, not ambivalent.

But on a tightrope, for sure.

And it is so hard.

My morning writing meditation both helps me walk that tightrope… and underscores how very, very taut it is.

How easily I can fall off.

(…and that's how it ends that day. But what a downer. No. Let's not finish yet. Let's walk on… Re-adjust the straps on your shoes, beloved. Suffer with me, for me, just a little longer.)

V.

It's another day of writing on the couch, my near-five-year-old tucked into my armpit, *Blue's Clues* in the background again, and an intermittent plea "You said you'd make jellyroll today!" impinging on my flow.

247

I am negotiating, compromising, walking the tightrope. I do not write in the kitchen, where I am theirs to access. I get that. I have that space-that-is-me-my-heart-mind-made-into-place, the place where I work and draft... That is also where I would like to write-meditate in the mornings.

But...

Mommy? Could you please, please sit with me on the couch? I need you to be near me!

And so, I give him my physical self.

My mind writes. It is absent from him.

It is... an imperfect practice. My elder children (I hope) understand what I am doing and why it is so important to me (if they don't quite understand, they accept). The little one does not. He knows-sees that I'm not fully there for him, and his ability to deal is varied. Sometimes, he will settle for being just near me. And sometimes, he desperately wants more.

Jellyroll? When are we going to make the jellyroll? Mom? Move your arm! Mom! Help me! I'm stuck in the crack!

There's an edge of resentment to my flow. And also— urgency. I write, sketch, chase ideas, nail down phrases, developments as quickly as possible. Because, at any point, any one of those,

Mooom! Help me!

...might be the last.

Meditation? Ha. Maybe that's not what most people understand by meditation. But it's the best I can do right now.

VI.

I commit in this piece the biggest blogging sin: I'm writing about me, *it's all about me*, instead of telling you the "Ten Surefire Ways to Achieve World Peace, Eternal Happiness, and Total Creative Fulfillment By Friday."

Next week, I'll make it all about you. I promise.

But right now? I've just wrenched a four-hour block of time from life, and I'm going to go use it.

Don't you dare interrupt me.

I love you and I can't imagine life without you. Except when I'm writing. Then I just need you to go away—and let me write.

xoxo
"Jane"

PS Next week, "Ten Surefire Ways to Achieve World Peace, Eternal Happiness, and Total Creative Fulfillment By Friday." Or something like that.

PS2 You can slip those shoes off now. But put them back on if you decide to re-read the post. Trust me. It's a totally different experience in bare feet.

PS3 Vera Pavloa's poetry collection *If There Is Something To Desire* is available in a fabulous English translation, and it may change your life.

USEFUL THING 3:
Ten Surefire Ways to Achieve World Peace, Eternal Happiness, and Total Creative Fulfillment By Friday

1. DON'T CLICK on, and for goddsake, don't READ, anything called "Ten Surefire Ways to Achieve World Peace, Eternal Happiness, and Total Creative Fulfillment by Friday."

2. ...
    ...
    ...

Yeah, I got nothing else.

But I'm pretty sure I just gave you an immense gift of time. What are you going to go do with it?

xoxo
"Jane"

USEFUL THING 4:
Resources, references, and all the links compiled in one place

REFERENCES TO THE books, authors, sites, quotes etc. mentioned in the main text. In order of my opinion of their usefulness to you. Also known as a bibliography.

FIRST, CHERYL STRAYED:
The Cheryl Strayed Interview on Long Form: soundcloud.com/longform/longform-podcast-144-cheryl-srayed (yes, there's a 't' missing from the URL)

Maria Popova's transcription of the "most shimmering parts" of the above podcast: BrainPickings.org/2015/06/15/cheryl-strayed-longform-podcast-interview/

Cheryl Strayed's "Write Like a Motherfucker" essay, on *The Rumpus*: TheRumpus.net/2010/08/dear-sugar-the-rumpus-advice-column-48-write-like-a-motherfucker/

Cheryl Strayed, *Tiny Beautiful Things: Advice on Life and Love by Dear Sugar* (Vintage, 2012)

IF YOU WANNA WRITE…

Julia Cameron, *The Artist's Way* (TarcherPerigee, 2002); for more resources from Cameron, check out her website at juliacameronlive.com. Of all of her offerings, *The Artist's Way* is the most important, but I also really love *How To Avoid Making Art (and anything else you enjoy)* (TarcherPerigee, 2005), as well as *Walking In This World* (TarcherPerigee, 2003)

Anne Lamott, *Bird By Bird* (Anchor, 2007)

Maria Popova, "Anne Lamott on Writing And How Perfectionism Kills Creativity," BrainPickings.org/2013/11/22/bird-by-bird-anne-lamott/

Maria Popova, "9 Books On Reading and Writing," BrainPickings.org/2012/01/09/best-books-on-writing-reading/

—and pretty much anything and everything on Popova's BrainPickings.org

Natalie Goldberg, *Writing Down the Bones: Freeing The Writer Within* (Shambhala, 2016)

SARK, *Juicy Pens, Thirsty Paper: Gifting the World with Your Words and Stories, and Creating the Time and Energy to Actually Do It* (Harmony, 2008)

Dan Millman and Sierra Prasada, *The Creative Compass: Writing Your Way from Inspiration to Publication* (H J Kramer, 2013)

Sarah Selecky on SarahSelecky.com for courses, writing prompts and inspiration

ON SELLING DA' WRITING

Austin Kleon, *Share Your Work: 10 Ways to Share Your Creativity and Get Discovered* (Workman Publishing Company, 2014) and *Steal Like An Artist: 10 Things Nobody Told You About Being Creative* (Workman Publishing Company, 2012)—I don't go into Kleon's at all in this book, but, fuck, yeah, read it, learn from it—plus, it's tiny, visual and perfect for anyone with ADD or "not enough time" syndrome

Jennifer Lee, *The Right-Brain Business Plan* (New World Library, 2011) and *Building Your Business The Right-Brain Way* (New World Library, 2014); her website, RightBrain BusinessPlan.com, is also full of practical and playful resources

The Kleon and Lee sources above are the ones I think you'll benefit from the most. I reference the below resources in this book, and they won't do you harm, but I don't think they'll change your life:

Canadian Writer's Market, edited by Heidi Waechtler (McClelland & Stewart; 19th Revised, Updated Edition, 2013)

Novel and Short Story Writer's Market, edited by Rachel Randall (Writer's Digest Books, 2014); if you're going to get any 'Market' book, get the most current version. Better yet, just use the Internet...

Get Started In Writing and Selling Erotic Fiction, by Judith Watts & Mirren Baxeter (Hodder & Stoughton, 2013)—for the record, three years later, I still haven't actually read this book except for page 230 & 231 of the Appendix: 'Publishers—the big trade houses' and 'Specialist and independent publishers.' But for that content alone, it was worth getting!

Writer's Digest Editors' Guide to Writing a Synopsis: writersdigest.com/editor-blogs/guide-to-literary-agents/synopsis-writing

My Break-The-Rules Synopsis: mjanecolette.com/tell-me-the-official-synopsis

Sell Yourself Without Selling Your Soul: a woman's guide to promoting herself, her business, her product, or her cause with integrity and spirit, by Susan Harrow (Harper Paperbacks, 2003)—this is not a bad book, but for a writer in the digital age, dated

sources for the POETRY and QUOTES
Irving Layton, *The Whole Bloody Bird* (McClelland& Stewart, 1969)

J. Jack Halberstam, *Gaga Feminism: Gaga Feminism: Sex, Gender, and the End of Normal* (Beacon Press, 2012); also check out Halberstam's blog at jackhalberstam.com

Erica Jong, *Seducing the Demon: Writing For My Life* (TarcherPerigee, 2007)

Ernest Hemingway, *Selected Letters, 1917-1961* (edited by Carlos Baker; Scribner, 1984)

Ernest Hemingway, *A Moveable Feast* (Bantam Books, 1964)

Susan Sontag, *As Consciousness Is Harnessed to Flesh: Journals and Notebooks, 1964-1980* (Picador, 2013)

Sylvia Plath, "Mad Girl's Love Song," *The Collected Poems* (Harper Perennial Modern Classics, 2008)

Sylvia Plath, *Letters Home: Correspondence 1950-1963* (Harper Row, 1975)

Sylvia Plath, *Ariel: The Restored Edition: A Facsimile of Plath's Manuscript, Reinstating Her Original Selection and Arrangement* (Harper Perennial Modern Classics, 2005)

Gloria Steinem, *My Life On The Road* (Random House, 2015)

Hafiz, *The Gift: Poems by Hafiz, the Great Sufi Master*, interpreted by Daniel Ladinsky (Penguin Compass, 1999)

Hafez, Jahan Malek Khatun & Obayd-e Zakani, *Faces of Love: Hafez and the Poets of Shiraz*, translated by Dick Davis (Penguin Classics, 2013)

Hafiz, *The Tangled Braid: Ninety-Nine Poems by Hafiz of Shiraz*, translated by Jeffrey Einboden and John Slater (Fons Vitae, 2010)

Thomas Wolfe, *Letters To His Mother* (C. Scribner's Sons, 1943)

Karley Sciortino, "Why we like having sex with artists," (*Vulture*, December 19, 2014)

Vera Pavlova, *If There is Something to Desire: One Hundred Poems* (Knopf, 2012)

Poetry-Chaikhana.com: great starting point for Sufi and other sacred poetry in general

PoetryFoundation.org: best starting point for getting into all sorts of poetry

JUST FOR FUN

Erotic Astrology: The Sex Secrets of Your Horoscope Revealed by Phyllis Vega (Adams Media, 2009)—it's really funny; the Calgary Public Library has a copy and so might yours, and you should totally check it out

Sextrology: The Astrology of Sex and the Sexes by Stella Starsky and Quinn Cox (William Morrow Paperbacks, 2004)

The Joy of Sex: The timeless guide to lovemaking by Alex Comfort and Susan Quilliam—assortment of new and revised editions; I think the original 1975 is so worth flipping through

The Whole Lesbian Sex Book: A Passionate Guide for All of Us by Felice Newman (Cleis Press, 2004)

The Complete Kama Sutra: The First Unabridged Modern Translation of the Classic Indian Text by Alain Daniélou (translator) (Inner Traditions, 1993)

Vagina: Revised & Updated by Naomi Wolf (Ecco, 2013)—for the record, I found this book infuriating, and I'm including it here chiefly because "vagina: revised & updated" looks hilarious. Also, the word, Naomi, is VULVA unless you're just talking about the hole. Which you're not. (See, three years after I read it, *Vagina* is still pissing me off)

Cunt: A Declaration of Independence by Inga Muscio (Seal Press, 2009)—read this instead of *Vagina*

MYSTERIES
Who is Leslie McIntyre?

Where, exactly, does this George Jean Nathan quote—"Art is the sex of the imagination"—come from?

BY THE WAY

If you want a free e-copy of *CUNT versus PUSSY: an incomplete CONFESSION in rough DRAFT*, complete with live hyperlinks, and access to its behind-the-scenes, evolving on-line version, connect with me at:

mjanecolette.com/TellMe

EPILOGUE:
Math sucks, but it doesn't matter

October 4, 2016: I get mail.

Two envelopes, one big, one small.

In the small envelope is a cheque from a Toronto-based public relations agency. A beautiful, fat cheque for... about six hours worth of work—ok, call it eight, maybe even ten, if you include the time spent in the shower thinking about the project and the back-and-forth flurry of revisions-clarifications.

Also, it arrives in my mailbox about seven days after I've done the work.

There is much rejoicing in the household, for the housing charge and the visa bill will be paid.

In the big envelope is my royalty statement from HarperCollins.

No, you don't want to know.

There's a blue stamp; it says:

> *"TOO SMALL TO PAY - WILL*
> *BE CARRIED FORWARD TO*
> *NEXT ACCOUNTING."*

To cry or to drink?

A smart person—you know this is true—would make the obvious decision. The math is blindingly obvious.

The stupid writer sighs... and writes some more.

ABOUT THE AUTHOR:
evolution of a bio

m jane colette's left-brain persona sold out long ago. She wears severely-cut suits of black, blue, and only that shade of green ("No, not that shade—have you seen the colour of my hair and eyes? Please. Let's coordinate.") and spends a lot of time in board rooms, offices, and "war rooms" (what a name!) parsing lies. It's a living.

(But, oh, what a plethora of source material...)

Her right-brain persona longs to be an iconoclast and an artist. When nobody's looking, she writes poetry.

Tell Me is her left side's and right side's first collaboration.

What's with this talking about yourself in the third person thing?
—My therapist says it's a coping-defensive-distancing technique. But it doesn't do a lot of harm.

You sure? Cause it's kind of creepy.
—Don't judge me.

They're both inordinately fond of parentheses, em-dashes and non-sequiturs.

Left: It's how you knock 'Them' off-balance, before you move in for the kill.

259

Right: It's how you defy the grammar-unartists and let language sing.

They have the same taste in shoes.

Left: It's more of a fetish.
Right: Definitely a fetish. And not a cheap one. That's why I let her sell out, by the way.

They're overwhelming and exhausting.

I bet.
—You don't know the half of it.

Their second novel, *Consequences* (unless you tell them to change the title to *Defensive Adultery*), is coming Spring 2017.

Left: What?
Right: Who's writing it?
Left: This is something you really should discuss with us in advance.
Right: Yeah. We're busy! Things to do, shoes to buy…
Left: Mmmm, shoes…

Don't worry. They already wrote it.

Right: Then why isn't it available in stores and on Amazon yet?
Left: Delayed gratification, gurrl, you ever heard of that?

Exhausting. But they give a hell of an interview, don't you think? You can get to know either/both of them better at:

@mjanecolette
tellme@mjanecolette.com
facebook.com/mjanecolette2
goodreads.com/mjanecolette
mjanecolette.com/TellMe